me ref £41.75

ARMY RECORDS
FOR
FAMILY HISTORIANS

BY

SIMON FOWLER

D1355523

PRO Publications,
Public Record Office, Chancery Lane,
London WC2A 1LR

Crown copyright 1992

ISBN 1 873162 04 9

LIST OF ILLUSTRATIONS

	Page
A class list	65
The Army List	66
Hart's Army List	67
Commanders in chief memoranda (WO 25/1048)	68
Officer's service record (WO 76/261)	69
Soldiers' documents (WO 97/1)	70
Description book (WO 25/351)	71
Muster roll (WO 10/2086)	72
Deserters (WO 25/2935)	73
Admission books, Royal Hospital Chelsea (WO 116/2)	74
Admission books, Royal Hospital Kilmainham (WO 119/1)	75
Medal roll (WO 100/46)	76
Award of Victorian Cross (WO 98/4)	77
Nurses' testimonials (WO 25/264)	78
War diaries (WO 95/2654)	79
Rolls of honour (RAIL 527/993)	80

Cover

Men of 'B' company, the Devonshire Regiment, in trenches during the South African War c1901 ref: WO 108/341

CONTENTS

1. PREFACE   1

2. USING THE RECORDS   1

3. ORGANIZATION OF THE ARMY   2
    3.1 Before 1660   2
    3.2 1660-1750   2
    3.3 1750-1870   2
    3.4 1870-1945   3
    3.5 The regiment   3
    3.6 Location of units   4
    3.7 Higher command   5
    3.8 Ranks   5

4. GENERAL GENEALOGICAL RECORDS   6
    4.1 Registers of births, marriages and deaths   6
    4.2 Casualties   7
    4.3 The census   8
    4.4 Wills   8

5. RECORDS OF THE ARMY BEFORE 1660   8
    5.1 Muster Rolls   8
    5.2 Records before 1660   9

6. COMMISSIONED OFFICERS   9
    6.1 Introduction   9
    6.2 Army Lists   10
    6.3 Other lists   11
    6.4 Commissions, appointments, transfers and promotions   12
    6.5 Purchase of commissions   12
    6.6 Records of Service   13
        War Office Compilations   13
        Regimental service records   14
        Further information and miscellaneous series   14
    6.7 Half Pay and Pensions   14
        Half Pay   14
        Retired full pay   15
        Pensions for wounds   15
        Widows' pensions   16
        Children's and dependent relatives' allowances   16
    6.8 Summary of records   17

7. OTHER RANKS, 1660-1913   17
    7.1 Introduction   17
    7.2 Identifying a regiment   17

7. OTHER RANKS, 1660-1913 - continued
   7.3 Service records 18
     Soldiers' documents 18
     Additional series of service records 19
     Purchase of discharge 19
     Description books 19
   7.4 Pay Lists and Muster Rolls 20
   7.5 Deserters 20
   7.6 Women in the Army 21
   7.7 Pension records 22
     Administration of pensions 22
     Out-pensions 22
     Admission books 22
     Regimental registers 23
     Pension returns 23
     In-pensions 23
     Pensions: other sources 24
   7.8 Soldiers settling abroad 24
   7.9 Summary of records 24

ROYAL ARTILLERY 25
   8.1 Introduction 25
   8.2 Officers 25
   8.3 Other ranks 25
   8.4 Royal Horse Artillery 26

ROYAL ENGINEERS 26
   9.1 Introduction 26
   9.2 Officers 26
   9.3 Other ranks 27

10. MILITIA AND VOLUNTEERS 27
   10.1 Introduction 27
   10.2 Officers 28
   10.3 Other ranks 28
   10.4 Further information 29

11. MEDALS AND AWARDS, 1793-1913 29
   11.1 Introduction 29
   11.2 Campaign medals 29
   11.3 Long service and good conduct medals 30
   11.4 Gallantry medals 30
   11.5 Mentions in Despatches 31

12. COURTS MARTIAL 31
   12.1 Introduction 31

12. COURTS MARTIAL - continued
    12.2 Officers   32
    12.3 Other ranks   32
    12.4 Other sources   33

13. THE BRITISH ARMY IN INDIA AND THE INDIAN ARMY   33
    13.1 Introduction   33
    13.2 East India Company and Indian Army   33
    13.3 British Army in India   34
    13.4 Other sources   34

14. COLONIAL AND DOMINIONS FORCES   34
    14.1 Introduction, 1754-1902   34
    14.2 Records of individual colonial regiments   35
    14.3 North America, 1746-1783   35
    14.4 South Africa, 1899-1902   36
    14.5 1902-1953   36

15. FOREIGN TROOPS IN BRITISH PAY   37
    15.1 Introduction   37
    15.2 1775-1816   38
    15.3 King's German Legion   38
    15.4 1815-1854   39
    15.5 The Crimean War   39
    15.6 Second World War   39

16. RECORDS OF ANCILLARY SERVICES   40
    16.1 Barrackmasters   40
    16.2 Chaplains   40
    16.3 Civilian employees   41
    16.4 Commissariat   41
    16.5 Invalids and Veterans   41
    16.6 Medical services   42
    16.7 Nursing services   43
    16.8 Ordnance Office   44
    16.9 Ordnance Survey   44
    16.10 Prisoners of war (POWs)   45
      Pre-1914   45
      First World War   45
      Second World War   45
      Korea   46
    16.11 Royal Marines   46
    16.12 Schools and Colleges   46

17. FIRST WORLD WAR   47
    17.1 Background reading   47
    17.2 Service records   47

FIRST WORLD WAR - continued
    Officers   47
    Other ranks   47
    17.3 Casualty records   48
    17.4 Medical and disability records   48
    17.5 Medal rolls   48
    17.6 War Diaries   49
    17.7 Royal Flying Corps   49
    17.8 Conscientious objectors   50
    17.9 Women in the war   50

SECOND WORLD WAR   50
    18.1 Service records   50
    18.2 Casualty returns   51
    18.3 War diaries   51
    18.4 Home Guard   52
    18.5 Medals   52
    18.6 Women in the war   52

OTHER TWENTIETH CENTURY CAMPAIGNS
AND THE PEACETIME ARMY   53
    19.1 War diaries   53
    19.2 Quarterly Historical Reports   53

PENDIX 1 ORGANIZATIONAL CHART OF THE ARMY   54

PENDIX 2 RANKS OF THE BRITISH ARMY   55

PENDIX 3 USEFUL DATES   56

PENDIX 4 RECORDS HELD BY OTHER INSTITUTIONS   59
    Local record offices   59
    Imperial War Museum   59
    British Library, Oriental and India Office Collections
      (formerly India Office Library and Records (IOLR))   60
    National Army Museum   60
    Regimental museums   61
    Office of Population Censuses and Surveys
      (General Register Office)   61
    Scotland   62
    Ireland   62
    Society of Genealogists   63

PENDIX 5 FURTHER READING   63

.USTRATIONS   65

)EX   81

1. PREFACE

The Public Record Office (PRO) holds many sources of great importance to family historians who had ancestors serving in the British Army. This Readers' Guide is a revision of *Records of Officers and Soldiers who have served in the British Army*, published by the PRO in 1986. A number of new sections and appendices have been added, in particular to take account of the growth of interest in records of the two world wars.

This book describes the main series of records of the War Office and other government departments which provide information about officers and soldiers who have served in the British Army. Almost all War Office records give some information about individuals, but this guide concentrates on those series containing material of greatest potential interest to the family historian. Most of the records described here are at the Public Record Office in Kew. Where they are at the PRO Chancery Lane this is noted in the text.

The Readers' Guide could not have been written without the assistance of Tim Anderson, Susan Healy, Liz Hallam-Smith, Douglas Hendry, Norman Holding, Hilary Jones, Michael Jubb, Alfred Knightbridge, John Peatty, Melvyn Stainton and Garth Thomas.

2. USING THE RECORDS

The Public Record Office houses many millions of documents. To trace the information you want, you need to know how they are arranged and how to use the various finding aids to them.

The system used by the PRO is relatively simple. The records are divided into 'classes', reflecting as far as possible their original administrative arrangement. Each class has its own title and identifying code, and consists of individual 'pieces' (usually a single document, but sometimes more). To order a piece you must know its complete reference. This is made up of letters and numerals: a lettercode (eg WO for War Office), a class number (eg WO 97 for War Office, Royal Hospital Chelsea, Soldiers' Documents) and a piece number (eg WO 97/341 for War Office, Royal Hospital Chelsea, Soldiers' Documents, 13th Foot, Abb-Car, 1760-1854). Individual pieces are briefly described in class lists, copies of which are to be found in the reference rooms at Kew and Chancery Lane (see example on page 65). Some lists have been published by the Public Record Office. Probably the most useful of these publications is the *Alphabetical Guide to War Office and other military records preserved in the Public Record Office* (PRO Lists and Indexes LXIII, 1931, reprinted 1963).

In addition, there are various other finding aids. A simple account of the means of reference available at the PRO can be found in Amanda Bevan and Andrea Duncan, *Tracing your ancestors in the Public Record Office* (4th edition, HMSO, 1990).

War Office records are described in some detail in the Public Record Office *Current Guide*, which is arranged in three parts. Part One of the Guide consists of administrative histories of departments, including the War Office and its component parts (Section 704). Part Two contains a description of each class of records, including those of the War Office (lettercode WO). Part Three is an index to the other two parts. Copies of the *Current Guide* are available at the PRO, and also on microfiche in large reference libraries and local record offices.

Many older War Office records are also described in outline in the *Guide to the Contents of the Public Record Office* (HMSO, 1963, 1968), Vol II pp. 304-33 and Vol III pp. 128-9, although some of the information is now very out of date.

The PRO has published a number of leaflets on military records, a list of which appears in appendix 5 below.

3. ORGANIZATION OF THE ARMY

It is difficult to use military records for genealogical purposes without first gaining a very general idea of how the British Army was organized, and how this changed over the years.

3.1   Before 1660

Before the outbreak of the civil war in 1642 there was no regular standing army in England, although there had been a militia in various forms since Anglo-Saxon times. Regiments were raised to meet special requirements and were usually known by the names of the colonels who commanded them. There was no central organization of these regiments and therefore no systematic records were created for them. A description of the few records useful to the genealogist is given in section 5 below.

3.2   1660-1750

With the restoration of Charles II a standing army became a permanent feature of government. Its administration was the responsibility of the secretary at war, with the help of an established bureaucracy which slowly developed into the War Office. As a result records are somewhat fuller than for the period before 1660, although sparse compared with later periods.

Because of Parliamentary suspicion of a standing army, organization of the Army remained minimal until the 1750s. Regiments were created and abolished as necessary. In general, regiments owed allegiance as much to their commanding officers as to the monarch.

3.3   1750-1870

By the 1740s and 1750s the regiment was established as the basic unit in the Army. Each regiment of foot, that is the infantry, was given a regimental number which was used until the 1880s and informally for many years after. Lists of regiments and their numbers are given in a number of books including David Ascoli, *A companion to the British Army,*

1660-1983 (London, 1983) and F C Markwell and Pauline Saul, *The family historian's enquire within* (3rd edition, Federation of Family History Societies (FFHS), 1991). The organization of the Army, however, still remained a very loose affair. In the 1780s, after the American War of Independence, there were in effect four separate armies: the Regular army; the Board of Ordnance (which included the Royal Artillery and the Royal Engineers); the militia under the control of the Home Office; and the Volunteers which existed as a series of private clubs. A series of reforms in 1855 gave the War Office responsibility for all military matters. As a result the Board of Ordnance was abolished and all its responsibilities passed to the War Office.

3.4   1870-1945

The Cardwell army reforms of the early 1870s radically reorganized the administration of the War Office, and in 1881 the whole structure of regiments was greatly changed. Each regiment was now linked to a county. Local militia forces, which had been autonomous, became the third battalion of the regiment. The use of numbers to identify foot regiments was discontinued. For a description of the organization of a regiment see section 3.5 below.

These reforms, however, did nothing to improve the machinery by which the Army was serviced and supplied, at home or in the field, although it is from this period that serious attention was first paid to the commissariat and to medical services. In addition, no reform was made of the Royal Artillery or cavalry regiments.

The Haldane reforms of 1907 to 1912 altered the central organization of the Army, creating a General Staff, under a chief of imperial general staff, to direct military operations. In addition, an expeditionary force of six infantry battalions and six cavalry regiments was formed. This force could be mobilized within twelve days and was the nucleus of the 'Old Contemptibles' of 1914.

The slimming down of the British Army after 1945 has led to further amalgamations and changes. These are covered in David Ascoli's book.

3.5   The regiment

The basic unit in the British Army is the regiment. The regiments were, and are, of various types: cavalry, infantry, artillery and engineer. They grew out of irregular units raised privately by noblemen and others to fight certain campaigns or battles. Before the reforms of the 1870s the terms battalion and regiment were used interchange- ably to describe the organization of the infantry. The term used depended on whether a regiment had one or two battalions: on paper an infantry regiment was composed of one battalion of ten to twelve companies, each of which had one hundred men. In theory, the strength of a regiment was about 1000 men, but in practice the average strength was usually between 600 and 800 men.

A company was commanded by a captain and two subalterns, who were lieutenants or second lieutenants. A regiment's senior officers were a colonel, a post which was usually honorific, a lieutenant colonel and two majors. Before 1871 these officers purchased

3

their commissions. Further details about this are given in section 6.5 below.
Administratively a regiment was divided into a depot and a service arm. The depot acted as the regimental headquarters and recruited and trained men for service. Before 1881 the depot moved quite frequently within the British Isles, but rarely went overseas. Depot companies were also responsible for quelling civil disturbances at home. The service companies were formed into a battalion commanded by a lieutenant colonel and served as the fighting unit of the regiment.

In 1881 reforms led to the merging of all but the first twenty-five regiments of the line (the infantry regiments) into bigger regiments of two or more battalions. These regiments were given territorial affinity to a regimental district, usually based on a county or city, with a depot or brigade headquarters in the county town. Locations of depots are given in the Army Lists, described in section 6.2 below.

The first battalion of a regiment was often stationed overseas while the second remained at home at the depot. Each regiment also had attached to it one or more battalions of volunteer militia.

During the two world wars the numbers of recruits, mainly conscripts, increased many times and up to ten extra battalions were formed for each regiment.

Cavalry regiments were slightly different in composition. A regiment of horse consisted of between six and eight troops of fifty men each. Each troop was commanded by a captain and subalterns. Cavalry regiments were reorganized in a similar manner to their infantry counterparts in 1922.

Battalions were identified by a number which could take several different forms, such as:

   1st Dorsets (ie 1st Battalion Dorsetshire Regiment)

   5th Grenadiers (5th Battalion Grenadier Guards)

   1/4 East Lancs (1st Line Territorials of the 4th Battalion East Lancashire Regiment)
A brief history of each regiment, together with a list of the principal campaigns and battles it fought, is given in Arthur Swinson (ed), *Register of the Regiments and Corps of the British Army* (London, 1972).

3.6   Location of units

There are several ways to locate the whereabouts of a regiment or battalion. The location of each battalion is given in the Monthly Army Lists, with the exception of the period between 1914 and 1918.

Another helpful source is the monthly returns which are in classes WO 17 and WO 73 (for a description of PRO references see section 2 above). The returns in WO 17 cover the period between 1759 and 1865, those in WO 73 are for 1859 to 1914. Both classes consist of returns to the adjutant general showing the distribution of each regiment at home and abroad, and its effective strength for all ranks.

From 1866 onwards the information contained in the monthly returns has been abstracted and printed in the *Annual Returns of the Army* which are in Parliamentary Papers and are available at Kew. Returns for 1750 and 1751 are in WO 27/1-2. A summary of returns is published in John M. Kitzmiller II, *In search of the 'forlorn hope': a comprehensive guide to locating British regiments and their records, 1640 to World War One* (Salt Lake City, 1988).

Orders of battle also contain lists of units, and give their location and their place in the command structure. Those for the First World War are in WO 95/5467-5494, and those for the Second World War in WO 212. Other orders of battle from 1939 are in WO 33.

3.7 Higher command

During wartime, regrouping of regiments and other units took place for operational purposes. Although still part of their parent regiments, battalions (usually four in number) were grouped together to form a brigade. Three brigades together formed a division. The division was a self-contained fighting force which, during both world wars, had its own artillery and support services. During the First World War, for example, its strength was about 20,000 men of all ranks.

Two, or sometimes more, divisions were grouped together as a corps. A group of two or more corps was designated as an army. It is customary to refer to armies in capital letters, ie THIRD ARMY; to corps with Roman numerals, eg XVI Corps; and to divisions with Arabic numerals, eg 30th Division. The term corps has two different meanings: as well as being a grouping of divisions it can mean a regiment of specialized troops, such as the Royal Artillery, (Royal) Army Service Corps or Royal Engineers. A simple organization chart for infantry regiments is in appendix 1 below.

3.8 Ranks

The Army comprised commissioned officers, usually from the wealthier classes, and other ranks, often drawn from the very poorest including paupers and criminals. Before the First World War it was very unusual for an ordinary soldier to become an officer. Very different sets of records grew up for officers and other ranks over the years. These records are as a result covered separately in this handbook, in sections 6 and 7 respectively below.

There was no uniform set of titles for the various ranks. Those used might reflect either the type of work performed or regimental custom. A list of ranks is given in appendix 2 below.

4. GENERAL GENEALOGICAL RECORDS

4.1 Registers of births, marriages and deaths

The PRO holds a small number of regimental registers of births, baptisms, marriages and burials. Some of these were annotated with information on discharge: others have baptismal entries for children entered on the same page as the marriage certificate of the parents.

The vast majority of records of births, marriages and deaths after 1837, however, are held by the Registrar General at St Catherine's House. A summary of the holdings is given in appendix 4 below.

Registers exist in the PRO for:

> 3rd battalion King's Own Yorkshire Light Infantry: baptisms and marriages, 1866-1904 (WO 68/499/1).
> 6th and 9th battalions, Rifle Brigade: baptisms and marriages, 1834-1904 (WO 68/439).
> Royal Artillery: marriages and baptisms, 1817-1827, 1860-1877 (WO 69/551-582).
> Royal Horse Artillery: baptisms and marriages, 1859-1877 (WO 69/63-73).
> 3rd and 4th battalions Somerset Light Infantry: baptisms and marriages, 1836-1887, 1892-1903 (WO 68/441).
> 3rd battalion West Norfolk Regiment: baptisms and marriages, 1863-1908 (WO 68/497).
> 3rd battalion Yorkshire Rifles: baptisms and marriages, 1832-1877 (WO 68/499).

In addition, there are registers of births at Dover Castle, 1865-1916 and 1929-1940; Shorncliffe and Hythe, 1878-1939; Buttervant, 1917-1922; and Fermoy, 1920-1921 in WO 156. WO 256 includes burial registers for the Canterbury garrison, 1808-1811, 1859-1884 and 1957-1958; and baptisms and banns of marriage for Army personnel in Palestine, 1939-1947.

Registers of baptisms, 1691-1812, marriages, 1691-1765, and burials, 1692-1856, for the Royal Hospital Chelsea are in RG 4/4330-4331, 4387 at Chancery Lane.

During the eighteenth and early part of the nineteenth centuries applicants for government jobs, including the Army, had to supply a certificate showing their place and date of baptism in order to prove their adherence to the Church of England. A collection of these certificates for officers extracted from other papers, and dating between 1777 and 1892, is in WO 32/8903-8920. Each piece is indexed. Similar series of certificates, again for officers only, of births, baptisms, marriages, deaths and burials, 1755-1908, extracted from War Office papers and files, are in WO 42; a name index is at the beginning of the class list.

Notifications to the War Office of marriages by officers, 1799-1882, are in WO 25/3239-3245.

4.2 Casualties

There are several series of monthly and quarterly casualty returns for both officers and ordinary soldiers, arranged by regiment, in WO 25. These returns are dated between 1809 and 1910 and many are indexed. They give name; rank; place of birth; trade; the date, place and nature of the casualty; debts and credits; and next of kin or legatee. The returns in WO 25/3250-3260 cover the period 1842-1872 and include details of men discharged or who had deserted.

A series of entry books of casualties, 1797-1817, from the Muster Master General's Office is in WO 25/1196-1358. These books give the names in alphabetical order with details of cause of death and any financial credits the deceased might have had.

Nominal rolls of casualties were kept for many of the campaigns in which the Army fought during the second half of the nineteenth century. These rolls include the names of officers as well as other ranks.

Campaign	Date	Reference
Burma	1888	WO 25/3473
China	1857-1858	WO 32/8221, 8224, 8227
	1860	WO 32/8230, 8233-8234
China (Tsingtao)	1915	WO 32/4996B
Egypt	1882, 1884	WO 25/3473
New Zealand	1860	WO 32/8255
	1863-1864	WO 32/8263-8268, 8271, 8276-8280
Sierra Leone	1898	WO 32/7630-7631
South Africa	1878-1881	WO 25/3474,
		WO 32/7700, 7706-7708, 7727, 7819
	1899-1902	WO 108/89-91, 338
Sudan	1884-1885	WO 25/3473.
		WO 32/6123, 6125-6126, 8382

Several casualty lists have been published: Frank and Andrea Cook, *The Casualty Roll for the Crimea* (London, 1976) and *South Africa Field Force Casualty List, 1899-1902* (London, 1972), the latter being a facsimile of WO 108/338. Copies of these books are available in the Reference Room at Kew.

Other records relating to casualties include registers of authorities to deal with effects, 1810-1822, in WO 25/2966-2971, an index to effects, 1830, in WO 25/2974, and a register of effects and credits, 1830-1844, in WO 25/2975. Papers relating to Artillery and Engineer deaths and effects, 1824-1859, are in WO 25/2972-2973, 2976-2978. Records of casualties during the two world wars are covered in sections 17 and 18 below.

4.3 The census

Apart from 1941, population censuses have been taken every ten years since 1801, but few returns relating to individuals survive before 1841. Census returns for England, Wales, the Isle of Man, and the Channel Islands for 1841 (HO 107), 1851 (HO 107), 1861 (RG 9), 1871 (RG 10), 1881 (RG 11) and 1891 (RG 12) are at Chancery Lane. The records include returns for all officers, soldiers, and their families living in barracks or other military establishments on census night, normally the first Sunday in April. The returns give details of where a person was born, marital state, age and occupation. Census records are described more fully in PRO Census Information Leaflet 3, *Censuses of Population, 1801-1891*. A more detailed booklet especially aimed at the family historian is Susan Lumas, *Making use of the Census* (Public Record Office Readers' Guide No 1, 1992).

4.4 Wills

Wills of many men are in the casualty returns in WO 25, with a few wills for officers in WO 42. Wills for soldiers who died abroad, before 1858, are in the records of the Prerogative Court of Canterbury at Chancery Lane. Copies of wills after 1858 are at the Principal Registry of the Family Division, Somerset House, Strand, London WC2R 1LP. Further details are given in PRO Records Information Leaflet 31, *Probate Records*

5. RECORDS OF THE ARMY BEFORE 1660

5.1 Muster Rolls

From Anglo-Saxon times able bodied men aged from 16 to 60 were liable to perform military service within the county where they lived. From the reign of Henry VIII recurring fears of invasion led the government to take steps to raise and maintain the level of efficiency of the local forces by holding musters; that is, general or specific assemblies of the militia of a shire to enable the inspection of both men and equipment by the lord lieutenant, or by another local gentleman appointed as a commissioner for musters. They were held on the orders of the King's Council. Muster rolls, or certificates, were drawn up and from the 1540s were returned to the secretaries of state. Early muster rolls may contain lists of men mustered, while others may contain merely totals. They may give occupations of, and type of arms carried by, individuals. In 1569 the names and parishes of residence of those mustered were asked for. From that date onwards relatively few certificates held by the PRO contain lists of names, though substantial lists may be found in the deputy lieutenant's muster books held in local record offices.

There are no separate classes of muster rolls earlier than 1757. Before this date they must be sought among a number of classes of records, especially: E 36, E 101, E 315, SP 1, SP 2, SP 10, SP 12, SP 14, SP 16, SP 17 at Chancery Lane. They are described in Jeremy

Gibson and Alan Dell, *Tudor and Stuart Muster Rolls* (FFHS, 1989). Most muster rolls are held in local record offices and are listed in Gibson and Dell. A number of muster rolls have been transcribed and subsequently published by local record societies.

For the militia records after 1757 see section 10 below.

5.2   Records before 1660

There was no central administration of the Army before 1660. Such references as there are to individual soldiers should be sought amongst the State Papers Domestic and State Papers Foreign (SP classes), and the Exchequer and Audit Accounts (AO 1 - AO 3): the regimental index in the *Alphabetical Guide to War Office records*, mentioned in section 2 above, is a good place to start. Other places to look are Exchequer Issues (E 403) and Exchequer Various Accounts (E 101) for the payment of military wages, the State Papers for widows' pensions, the licenses to pass beyond the seas (E 157) for oaths of allegiance taken by soldiers going to the Low Countries, 1613-1624, and the Commonwealth Exchequer Papers for the Army during the Interregnum (SP 28). With the exception of the Audit Office (AO) classes, these records are at Chancery Lane. Although there are some lists of names in the Exchequer classes, these records are difficult to use so they may involve a long and painstaking search to find anything of use. A list of officers who served in cavalry and infantry regiments during the Civil War is in Edward Peacock, *The Army List of Roundheads and Cavaliers* (London, 1863). A copy of the second edition, published in 1874, is kept in the Reference Room at Kew.

6.   COMMISSIONED OFFICERS

6.1 Introduction

Records giving personal information about an army officer were created routinely upon the granting of a commission, promotion, resignation or his being placed upon the half-pay list, and occasionally at other stages in his career.

There were four sorts of commissioned officer:

1. General officers, who co-ordinated the efforts of the whole army. They had the rank of field marshal, general, lieutenant general and major general.
2. Regimental officers, who commanded a regiment that is, colonel, lieutenant colonel and major.
3. Company officers, who were in charge of units within a regiment; that is, captain (in command of a company) and his subalterns, lieutenant, cornet (in the cavalry), ensign (infantry). In 1871 cornets and ensigns became second lieutenants.
4. Others: paymasters, adjutants, quartermasters, surgeons and chaplains.

There were also some other ranks, such as brigadier general, colonel-commandant, and brigade-major, which were used in individual regiments and corps. Officers were graded by seniority, which ruled promotion within the regiment. If an officer was promoted out of sequence, he was given brevet rank, eg as a brevet-major. Some officers held two ranks at the same time: the regimental rank, which was higher and was usually a special appointment, and the army rank, which was the actual rank of his commission. This often occurred during the two world wars when vacancies at a higher rank had to be filled because of casualties.

A list of Army ranks is in appendix 2 below.

6.2 Army Lists

The broad outline of an officer's career should be fairly easy to discover from the Army Lists.

Brief details of army officers have been gathered together since 1702 and published in these Lists from 1740. Since 1754 the Lists have been published regularly and are available in large reference libraries. The earliest volumes, however, are very rare. Incomplete sets are available in the Reference Room at Kew.

There are complete record sets, with manuscript amendments, of the annual lists between 1754 and 1879, and of the quarterly lists from 1879 to 1900, in WO 65 and WO 66 respectively.

There are five distinct series of Army Lists:

1. **Annual Army Lists** date from 1754 to 1879 and are arranged by regiment. Volumes from 1766 are indexed. Engineer and artillery officers are included in the index from 1803 only. The series was replaced by a Quarterly Army List from June 1879. For an example see figure 2 on page 66.

2. **Monthly Army Lists** date from 1798 to June 1940 and are arranged by regiment. In addition, they include some idea of the location of each unit. Officers of colonial, militia and territorial units are included. The lists are indexed from 1867. After July 1939 the lists were given a security classification and not published and in 1940 they were replaced by the Quarterly Army List.

3. **Quarterly Army Lists** There are two separate series of quarterly lists:
   1879-1922. These lists have two distinctive features. Firstly, in addition to the regimental list (which was discontinued in 1908) they include a gradation list; that is, lists of officers in seniority order, with dates of birth and promotions. In addition, from April 1881 details of officers' war service are included. Between 1909 and 1922 these details appear in the January issue only. This series of the Quarterly List was replaced by Half Yearly Army Lists in 1923.
   July 1940-December 1950. Quarterly Army Lists were produced in place of the Monthly Army List from July 1940. They were classified documents and not published. Despite the new name, the lists continued to be produced monthly or bi-monthly until December 1943. From then on they were issued quarterly until January 1947. They are not regimental lists and do not include the gradation list or details of officers' war services. From April 1947, although still styled

the Quarterly Lists, they were published in April, August and December each year.
4. **Half Yearly Army Lists** exist for the period between 1923 and February 1950. They replaced and took a similar form to the Quarterly Army Lists. They were issued in January and July each year and included a gradation list of serving officers. The January issue also includes a list of retired officers. From 1939 they became a restricted publication. From 1947 they were issued annually in February.
5. **Army Lists and Army Gradation Lists** The Army List was revised in 1951, and now consists of three parts: part 1, a list of serving officers; part 2, a list of retired officers; part 3, a brief biography of officers called the Gradation List. Part 3 is a restricted publication, and is not available to the general public. Part 2 is now published only every four years.

6.3 Other lists

Details of officers granted commissions before 1727 can most easily be traced in Charles Dalton, *English Army Lists and Commission Registers, 1661-1714* (6 vols, London, 1892-1904) and *George I's Army, 1714-1727* (2 vols, London, 1910-1912). Copies of Dalton's books are available in the Reference Room at Kew.
The Military Register, published from 1768 to 1772 and in 1779, includes Army and marine officers. *The Royal Military Calendar*, published in 1820, contains service records for officers from field marshal down to major, who held the rank at the date of publication. The *Calendar*, however, contains no personal information or details of officers' families. These books are available in the Reference Room at Kew.
Lieutenant General Henry Hart started an unofficial army list in February 1839, in part to fulfil the need for a record of officers' war services which he felt were inadequately covered in the official Army List. He noted them meticulously in extensive footnotes. Hart's Army Lists cover the period between 1839 and 1915 and were issued quarterly. An annual volume which contained additional information was also published. Copies of the lists, and Hart's papers, are in WO 211. An incomplete set of Hart's lists between 1840 and 1882 is available in the Reference Room at Kew. For an example see figure 3 on page 67.
Lists of artillery officers were published in *List of Officers of the Royal Regiment of Artillery, 1716-June 1914* (3 vols, London, 1899, 1914). A similar list was compiled for the Royal Engineers: *Roll of Officers of the Corps of Royal Engineers from 1660 to 1898* (London, 1898). In addition, there is a published *List of Commissioned Medical Officers of the Army, 1660-1960* (2 vols, 1925, 1968). These books are available in the Reference Room at Kew.
General staff officers and War Office staff (including civilian employees) are listed in the *War Office List* published by the War Office itself between 1861 and 1964.
A few manuscript lists of army officers between 1702 and 1823 may be found in WO 64 and there is a manuscript index to entries in the Army Lists between 1704 and 1765 in the Reference Room at Kew.

6.4 Commissions, appointments, transfers and promotions

Officers held their rank by virtue of a royal commission. The issue of a commission, or warrant of appointment, is likely to be recorded in several places. A small collection of original commissions between 1780 and 1874 is in WO 43/1059.

Warrants for the issue of commissions, between 1679 and 1782, can be found in the military entry books in the State Papers (SP 44/164-418) at Chancery Lane. They are continued between 1782 and 1855 in HO 51.

Commission books, kept by the secretary at war and the secretary of state for war between 1660 and 1803, are in WO 25/1-121. Similar information can be found in the notification books of the secretary at war, 1704-1858 (WO 4/513-520, WO 25/122-203).

Appointments and subsequent transfers and promotions are also recorded in the succession books of the secretary at war. They were compiled retrospectively from the notification and commission books. They are in two series:

by regiments	1754-1808	(WO 25/209-220)
by date	1773-1807	(WO 25/221-229).

Original submissions and entry books of submissions to the sovereign of recommendations for staff and senior appointments, rewards for meritorious service, and for commissions and appointments, 1809, 1871-1914, are in WO 103.

For artillery and engineer officers see sections 8 and 9 below.

6.5 Purchase of commissions

Before 1871 commissions were purchased, and promotion was generally by wealth rather than won by merit or experience. There were set prices for commissions, but they were widely exceeded. Once a commission had been purchased, officers were then able to buy up to the next rank as the opportunity presented. The whole system was widely condemned during the mid-Victorian period, and was finally abolished in 1871 by the Army Purchase Commission.

Applications to purchase and sell commissions, between 1793 and 1870, are in WO 31. Accompanying correspondence may also be included. These records are arranged chronologically by the date of appointment or promotion, usually in monthly bundles. These applications may shed considerable extra light on the individual concerned. The supporting documents often contain statements of service, certificates of baptism, and letters of recommendation. For an example see figure 4 on page 68.

Correspondence about the purchase and sale of commissions between 1704 and 1858 is contained in a series of indexed letter books in WO 4/513-520.

Hart's Army Lists note whether an officer bought his commission or not, and give the date when the purchase was made. Using this information it is thus possible to discover which bundle in WO 31 is likely to contain details of the purchase.

Both the official Army Lists and Hart's Army Lists record when an officer sold his commission. Unfortunately an exact date is not given, but the month or quarter can be determined.

Registers of service of every officer holding a commission on 1 November 1871 are in the papers of the Army Purchase Commission in WO 74, together with a series of applications from officers on the British and Indian establishments, 1871-1891, to which certificates of service are attached. Papers and applications are indexed by regiment but not by name of applicant.

6.6 Records of Service

Records of service of officers held by the Public Record Office fall into two main groups: those compiled by the War Office and those compiled in regimental record offices.

The records described below are only for officers who had retired before the end of 1913. Records of service of officers who served in the First World War and later wars and campaigns are described in sections 17, 18 and 19 below.

War Office Compilations

The War Office did not begin to keep systematic records of officers' service until the early nineteenth century, having relied on records retained by regimental record offices. During the nineteenth century, however, the War Office compiled five series of statements of service based on returns made by officers themselves:

Reference	Dates	Notes
WO 25/744-748	1809-1810	Arranged alphabetically. Contains details of military service only.
WO 25/749-779	1828	Refers to service completed before 1828. Arranged alphabetically and gives the age at commission, date of marriage and children's births as well as military service. Related correspondence from officers, whose surnames begin with D to R only, is in WO 25/806-807.
WO 25/780-805	1829	Gives similar information to the second series. The Army List for 1829 serves as an index to it.
WO 25/808-823	1847	Completed by retired officers and refers to service completed before this date. It is arranged alphabetically and contains the same information as the second series.
WO 25/824-870	1870-1872	Includes a few returns before 1870 and after 1872. It is arranged by year of return and then by regiment.

An incomplete name index to service records in WO 25 is available in the Reference Room at Kew.

Regimental service records

Many regimental record offices kept their own records of service. Those records, which were eventually transferred to the War Office, are now in WO 76. They are arranged by regiment and cover service between 1764 and 1961. The information they contain varies a great deal, but generally increased in detail during the course of the nineteenth century. An incomplete card index to names of officers is available in the Reference Room at Kew. For an example see figure 5 on page 69.

Service records for officers in the Royal Garrison Regiment, 1901-1905, are in WO 19 and those of the Gloucester Regiment, 1792-1866, are in WO 67/24-27.

For artillery and engineer officers see sections 8 and 9 below.

Further information and miscellaneous series

A few papers and correspondence relating to individual officers are in WO 43. Particulars of service and some personal information for a small number of mainly senior officers, 1830-1961, can be found in a series of selected personal files in WO 138. These records are not available for public inspection until 75 years after the closure of the file.

A few confidential reports on officers, 1872-1905, are included in WO 27/489.

Inspection returns in WO 27, for the period 1750 to 1857, record the presence or absence of officers from their regiments at the time of inspection and may contain a brief record of service. The absence of officers is also recorded in the monthly returns, 1759-1865, in WO 17.

Additions to the list of general officers receiving unattached pay, that is, pay other than from their regiment, 1835-1853, are recorded in WO 25/3230-3231. Staff paybooks and returns, 1782-1870, are in WO 25/689-743. Ledgers of the payment of unattached pay, 1814-1896, are in PMG 3. Alphabetical registers of those receiving unattached pay, 1872-1880, are in WO 23/66-67.

A list of officers killed and wounded at the Battle of Waterloo is contained in Wellington's despatch of 29 June 1815, printed as a supplement to the *London Gazette* of 1 July 1815: copies can be found in ZJ 1/138 and MINT 16/111. A list of officers (and men) present during the siege of Fort Mary, Lydenburg, South Africa in 1881 is in WO 32/7820. A list of officers present during the siege of Ladysmith, South Africa in 1899-1900 is in WO 32/7114B.

6.6 Half Pay and Pensions

Half Pay

Not until 1871 were officers entitled to a pension as of right. Before then, officers who wished to retire either sold their commissions, recouping their capital investment, or went on to half pay. The system of half pay was set up in 1641 for officers of reduced or disbanded regiments. In time it became essentially a retaining fee, paid to officers so long as a commission was held; thus they were, in theory if not in practice, available for future service. From 1812 there was provision for its payment to officers unfit for service.

During the nineteenth century the system became more and more heavily abused. Officers who could afford to go onto half pay could avoid service abroad or any unwelcome posting. It was also possible to buy a commission and then go on half pay the next day, which made officers eligible to purchase the next commission up without serving any time with the regiment.

Registers of half pay officers are in WO 23. A series of alphabetical registers of those in receipt of half pay between 1858 and 1894, giving name, rank, regiment, date of commencement, rate and a record of payments, is in WO 23/68-78. These are often annotated with the date of the officer's death.

Ledgers recording the issue of half pay from 1737 to 1921 are in PMG 4. Until 1841 these are arranged by regiment and unindexed; thereafter they are arranged alphabetically by name. Deaths, the assignment of pay, and sales of commissions are noted in the ledgers, and from 1837 they give addresses. Later volumes also give dates of birth. Lists of those entitled to receive half pay between 1713 and 1809, arranged by regiment, are in WO 24/660-747. WO 25/2979-3002 contains further nominal lists, for the period 1712 to 1763, and registers of warrants for half pay between 1763 and 1856. Replies to a circular of 1854, with details of the fitness for service of half pay officers, may be found in WO 25/3009-3012. Further miscellaneous lists relating to half pay are in WO 25/3003-3008, 3013-3016.

Registers of half pay disbursed to officers living abroad are in WO 25/3017-3019; these cover the period 1815 to 1833. WO 25/3232 is a register of permissions granted to officers on half pay to be abroad between 1815 and 1833.

Claims from wounded officers for half pay between 1812 and 1858 are contained in a series of letterbooks in WO 4/469-493.

Officers receiving half pay are listed in the Army List.

Retired full pay

A few officers, mainly those with a letter of service for raising an invalid or a veteran corps, were entitled to retired full pay. Registers of those receiving such pay, 1872-1894, are included in WO 23/66-74. Further registers, 1830-1870, are in WO 25/3000-3004. Ledgers of payments, 1813-1896, are in PMG 3.

Registers of payments made to Army (and Royal Marines) officers in reduced circumstances between 1720 and 1738 are in WO 109/55-87.

Pensions for wounds

A system of pensions for wounded officers was set up in 1812. Registers of those who received such pensions, between 1812 and 1897, are in WO 23/83-92. Correspondence on claims between 1812 and 1855 is in WO 4. Other correspondence, 1809-1857, is in WO 43, for which there is a card index in the Reference Room at Kew. Ledgers for these payments, 1814-1920, are in PMG 9 .

Widows' pensions

Although officers had no entitlement to a pension, provision was made from 1708 for the payment of pensions to widows of officers killed on active duty. From 1818, fifteen annuities were also paid to widows of officers whose annual income did not exceed £30 a year out of a fund created by the will of Colonel John Drouly.
There are several series of registers of those receiving widows' pensions and the Drouly Annuities:

Reference	Dates	Notes
WO 24/804-883	1713-1829	
WO 25/3020-3050	1735-1769	Indexes,1748-1811, are in WO 25/ 3120-3123.
PMG 11	1808-1920	Not April 1870 - March 1882 (in PMG 10).
WO 23/105-113	1815-1892	
PMG 10	1870-1882	Continuation of PMG 11.

In addition, there are several series of application papers for widows' pensions and dependents' allowances:

Reference	Dates	Notes
WO 42	1755-1908	These papers may include proofs of birth, marriage, death and probate.
WO 25/3089-3197	1760-1810	Arranged alphabetically, with abstracts of the applications between 1808 and 1825 in WO 25/3073-3109. There is an index in the Reference Room at Kew.
WO 43	1818-1855	A few applications only.

Children's and dependent relatives' allowances

From 1720 pensions were also paid to children and dependent relatives of officers out of the Compassionate Fund and the Royal Bounty. Registers giving the names of those placed on the Compassionate List, 1779-1812 and 1815-1894, and recording the amounts they received are in WO 24/771-803 and WO 23/114-123. Applications for grants from the Fund, for 1812 and 1813 only, are in WO 25/3110-3114. Ledgers recording payment from both the Compassionate Fund and the Royal Bounty, 1840-1916, are in PMG 10. Correspondence relating to the Compassionate Fund, 1803-1860, is in WO 4/521-590.

6.8 Summary of records

To trace the service record of an officer in the Army you need to know his regiment, because the War Office kept no continuous central record of officers. The most important source for the career of an officer in the Army is the printed Army Lists. If your ancestor does not appear in these lists it is very unlikely that he was an officer. The Army Lists have been produced since 1740. They are arranged by regiment, and normally indexed after 1867. For further information see section 6.2 above. There are two main types of service record, those created by the War Office, which are in WO 25, and those produced by the regiments themselves, which are in WO 76. There are incomplete card indexes to these records in the Reference Room at Kew. Further information about them is in section 6.6 above.

7. OTHER RANKS, 1660-1913

7.1 Introduction

In the Army, the 'other ranks' were the privates (infantry) and troopers (cavalry), trumpeters and drummers, supervised by corporals and sergeants who were non-commissioned officers (NCOs) promoted from the ranks. Specialist corps and regiments, however, used different names. An outline of ranks in the Army is in appendix 2 below.

Before 1871 soldiers enlisted for a period of twenty-one years and served until they were disabled by wounds or old age. Discharges could be bought, but few had the money to do so. The Army Enlistment Act 1870 introduced a scheme whereby men could join the Army on a short-service engagement of twelve years, of which six would be spent with the colours and six on reserve. However, men could still re-engage for a maximum service of twenty-one years.

7.2 Identifying a regiment

To trace an ordinary soldier in the records you need to know the regiment in which he served, as records are arranged by regiment. If this information is unavailable there are still some possible ways of discovering the regiment.

It may be possible to identify the unit from old photographs. A useful article is D J Barnes, 'Identification and dating: military uniforms' in *Family history in focus*, ed. D J Steel and L Taylor (Guildford, 1984). There is also a chapter on the subject in Norman Holding, *More sources of World War I army ancestry* (FFHS, 1991). The registers of births of children of army personnel at St Catherine's House are indexed and it may be possible to determine a regiment from them, if you have some idea of when children were born or the area where a soldier served. For further details about these registers see appendix 4 below.

If you know the county or country in which your ancestor was living between 1842 and 1862 for England or Scotland, or between 1842 and 1882 for Ireland and abroad, you may be able to pinpoint the regiment from the records of payment of pensions in WO 22 and PMG 8, which include the names of regiments in which individuals served. For further details of these records see section 7.5 below.

If the soldier died in service, another possibility would be to check the records of soldiers' effects, which survive between 1810-1822, 1830-1844 and 1862-1881. They are in WO 25, arranged by initial letter of surname, and they give the regiment. This source is unlikely to be of use if the soldier died owing money to the Army.

If you have any idea about the place of service you may be able to identify the regiment from one of the sources listed in section 3.6 above.

7.3 Service records

Soldiers' documents

The most important records are attestation and discharge papers, forming the class known as soldiers' documents in WO 97, which cover the period between 1760 and 1913. Except for the early years, where the level of detail is limited, the documents give information about age, physical appearance, birthplace and trade or occupation on enlistment in the Army. They also include a record of service, including any decorations awarded, promotions and reductions in rank, crimes and punishments, and the reason for the discharge to pension. In some cases, place of residence after discharge and date of death are given. For an example see figure 6 on page 70.

These documents are arranged by discharge date. The order in many boxes has been considerably disturbed over the years so that it may mean looking through a whole box to find a particular individual.

The documents fall into four series:

1760-1854 These documents are arranged alphabetically by name within regiments, which is why it is vital to know the regiment in which a soldier served. There seem to be relatively few for men who enlisted before 1792. This series is available on microfilm in the Romilly Room at Kew.

1855-1872 These are again arranged alphabetically by name within a regiment, and it is vital to know the regiment in which a man served.

1873-1882 These are arranged alphabetically by name of soldier within the categories cavalry, artillery, infantry and corps.

1883-1913 This series covers both soldiers discharged to pension and those discharged for other reasons, such as the termination of limited engagements or discharge by purchase. The documents are arranged in surname order. Details of next of kin, wife and children are given.

The Public Record Office at present holds records of service only for *men discharged before 1914*. Records relating to the period after 1914 are covered in sections 17 to 19 below.

These service records are normally only for men who *were discharged and received a pension*. Soldiers' documents for soldiers who died whilst serving, or who did not receive a discharge certificate for any reason, have not survived.

Additional series of service records

Certificates of service similar to those in WO 97, for men discharged between 1787 and 1813 and awarded Chelsea out-pensions, are in WO 121/1-136. They are arranged in chronological order based on the date of the award of a pension.
General registers of discharges from 1871 to 1884 are in WO 121/223-238. Registers of men discharged without pension between 1884 and 1887 are in WO 121/239-257. Many of the pieces in WO 121 are in very poor condition and access to them may be restricted. Certificates of service of soldiers awarded deferred pensions, 1838-1896, are in WO 131.
Certificates of service for Irish soldiers awarded out-pensions by the Board of Kilmainham Hospital between 1783 and 1822 are in WO 119 (see also section 7.7 below). They are arranged by discharge number, which can be traced in the admission books in WO 118.
Two series of returns of service of NCOs and men survive from the early nineteenth century. The first series contains statements of periods of service and of liability to service abroad on 24 June 1806 (WO 25/871-1120). The second series contains returns of NCOs and men, not known to be dead or totally disqualified for military service, who had been discharged between 1783 and 1810 (WO 25/1121-1131). Both series are arranged by regiment and then alphabetically by surname.

Purchase of discharge

It was possible to buy discharge from the Army for the sum of £20, or less depending on the length of service. Registers, arranged by regiment, for the period 1817-1870 are in WO 25/3845-3868.

Description books

Description books give a description of each soldier, his age, place of birth, trade and service. There are two main series. The regimental description and succession books are in WO 25/266-688. They cover the period between 1778 and 1878, but not all the regiments' books start so early or go on so late; for most regiments there are volumes only for the first half of the nineteenth century. Some are arranged alphabetically, others by date of enlistment. For an example see figure 7 on page 71.
Similar books for a small number of regimental depots, 1768 to 1908, are in WO 67. Depot Description Books tend to be more complete, because they listed people as they joined, although they do not include men who transferred from one regiment to another.

7.4 Pay Lists and Muster Rolls

When the regiment in which a soldier served is known or has been ascertained from other records, the muster rolls and pay lists provide a comprehensive means of establishing his date of enlistment, his movements throughout the world and his date of discharge or death. The first entry may show his age on enlistment, as well as the place where he enlisted. An entry on the form 'men becoming non-effective', sometimes found at the end of each quarter's muster, shows the birthplace, trade and date of enlistment of any soldier discharged or dying during the quarter. From about 1868 to about 1883, at the end of each muster (or the beginning for regiments stationed in India), may be found a marriage roll, which lists wives and children for whom married quarters were provided. For an example see figure 8 on page 72.

The main series of muster books and pay lists are arranged by regiment and are bound in volumes covering a period of twelve months. They were compiled monthly. They are in the following separate classes for:

Unit	Dates	Class reference
Artillery	1708-1878	WO 10
Engineers	1816-1878	WO 11
Foreign Legions	1854-1856	WO 15
General	1732-1878	WO 12
Militia and Volunteers	1780-1878	WO 13
New series	1878-1898	WO 16
Scutari Depot	1854-1856	WO 14

WO 12 includes household troops, cavalry, Guards, regular infantry, special regiments and corps, colonial troops, various foreign legions and regiments, and regimental, brigade and other depots. WO 14 and WO 15 relate to troops engaged in the Crimean War.

WO 16 continues the material in classes WO 10 to WO 12, from 1888 as company muster rolls only, arranged chiefly by regimental districts. From 1882 arrangement of the musters in this class reflects the reorganization of the Army on a territorial basis. The Army Lists contain indexes to regiments with their regimental district numbers.

7.5 Deserters

Registers of deserters, 1811-1852, are in WO 25/2906-2934. Until 1827 these volumes consist of separate series for cavalry, infantry and militia (the latter up to 1820 only). After 1827 they are arranged in one series by regiment. They give descriptions, dates and places of enlistments and desertions, and may indicate what happened to deserters who were caught. For an example see figure 9 on page 73.

Registers of captured deserters, 1813-1848, with indexes to 1833, are in WO 25/2935-2954. They include registers of deserters who were caught or who surrendered, and give the name of the individual and his regiment; the date of his committal and place of confinement; what happened to him (that is, whether he returned to his regiment or was discharged from the Army); and the amount of the reward paid (if the man had not surrendered) and to whom paid.

Returns of deserters captured and held as prisoners on the Savoy Hulks, in the Thames Estuary, 1799-1823, are in WO 25/2956-2961. These returns are not indexed. Deserters who surrendered under proclamation between 1803 and 1815 are in WO 25/2955. Casualty returns in WO 25, described in section 4.2 above, list deserters as well as casualties. Miscellaneous correspondence relating to individual deserters, 1744-1813 and 1848-1858, is in WO 4/591-654.

The *Police Gazette* included in each issue a current list of men who had deserted from the Army (and Royal Marines), with a detailed description of each individual. Copies between 1828 and 1845 are in HO 75.

Information about deserters, 1716-1830, can also be found in the deserter bounty certificates in E 182. These record the payment of rewards to the captors of deserters. There is an incomplete card index to surnames of deserters. The records, and the index, are at Chancery Lane.

A list of deserters at large in Australia has recently been published in Yvonne Fitzmaurice, *Army deserters from HM Service* (vol 1, Forest Hill, Vic., 1988). A copy of this book is available in the Reference Room at Kew.

7.6 Women in the Army

Until women nurses were first recruited during the Crimean War, no woman formally served in the British Army. One or two, however, did enlist pretending to be men, although there are no separate records for these women. Six wives of soldiers in each company were carried on strength to act as unofficial cooks, laundresses and servants to officers. In addition, there were a large number of camp followers who, unlike the army wives, were not entitled to an issue of 'the King's victuals'. Little is known about these women.

There are very few records of these people. Wives of soldiers are recorded in the soldiers' discharge documents, in WO 97, from the 1850s onwards. Occasionally women retained on strength may appear in the muster rolls in WO 12.

7.7 Pension records

Administration of pensions

Originally pensions took the form of accommodation for disabled soldiers in the Royal Hospital Chelsea, which was established in 1690. Soldiers on the Irish establishment were accommodated at the Royal Hospital Kilmainham, established in 1679. These pensions became known as in-pensions.

Within a few months the accommodation became insufficient to meet the demand, and a system of out-pensions for non-residents was devised to supplement the original in-pensions. They could be claimed on the grounds of disability or unfitness arising from service. In the 1750s regulations were passed to make length of service and character the principal reasons for award of pensions, and not disability. Responsibility for the out-pensions of Irish pensioners passed to Chelsea in 1822, and for in-pensioners in 1929.

Except for a few officers admitted as in-pensioners, the two hospitals were not concerned with officers' pensions.

The major series of records created as a result was the soldiers' documents (WO 97) described in section 7.3 above. Additional information can be found in many further series.

For a brief account of both the Royal Hospitals see the PRO *Current Guide* Part 1, section 704/6/3.

Out-pensions

There are three main series of records containing information about out-pensioners admission books, regimental registers and pension returns. These series cover the vast majority of pensioners at home and abroad.

Admission books

These are arranged chronologically by date of examination for the award of an out pension, and are not indexed. Therefore you need to know at least the approximate date of the award of a pension before a search becomes practicable.

For pensions awarded by the Royal Hospital Chelsea, there are two series of admission books covering pensions awarded for disability, 1715-1913, in WO 116/1-124, 186 251. Details of pensions awarded for length of service, 1823-1913, are in WO 117. For pensions awarded by the Royal Hospital Kilmainham between 1704 and 1922 there is just one series in WO 118. For an example see figures 10 and 11 on pages 74 and 75. Each book gives the date of examination; a brief record of service; the reason why a pension was awarded; place of birth; and a physical description. Between 1830 and 1844 the Chelsea admission books are duplicated by registers in WO 23/1-16 where in addition the intended place of residence is given. The registers, 1838-1844, in WO 23/10-16 are indexed.

Regimental registers

These registers are for pensions issued at Chelsea, and are in two distinct series in WO 120. The first, 1715-1843, in WO 120/1-51 is arranged chronologically within regiments, and gives date of admission, age, a brief record of service, rate of pension, 'complaint', place of birth and a physical description. The volumes for 1839 to 1843 are indexed. In addition, a name index to some infantry regiments, 1806-1858, in WO 120/23-26, 29-30 is kept in the Reference Room at Kew.

The second series in WO 120/52-70 records pensions being paid between 1814 and 1857. Admissions before 1845 are arranged by rate of pension, those between 1845 and 1857 chronologically. The registers give rate of pension, date of admission and residence, and are marked up with the place of payment of the pension and date of death. These registers are duplicated and extended to 1876 in WO 23/26-65. A similar series of registers of pensions being paid from 1806 to 1807 is in WO 23/136-140.

Pension returns

Before 1842 out-pensions were paid by convenient local officials, such as excise officials. In 1842 payment was made the responsibility of staff officers of pensioners, in a number of districts. Each staff officer made a monthly return to the War Office in which he recorded pensioners who had moved into, or out of, his district, whose pension had ceased, or who had died. Pension returns in WO 22 record pensions paid or payable from district offices between 1842 and 1883.

These returns give the pensioner's name, regiment, rate of pension, date of admission to pension, rank, and the district to which, or from which, he had moved. Also included with the returns are various items of statistical information. Returns for British payment districts cease in 1862, but returns relating to pensions paid overseas and in the colonies extend into the 1880s.

In-pensions

There are muster rolls for in-pensioners of Chelsea Hospital (the men commonly called Chelsea Pensioners) for 1702-1789 in WO 23/124-131, and for 1864 and 1865 in WO 23/132. A list of in-pensioners, 1794-1816, is in WO 23/134. There is an alphabetical register, 1837-1872, in WO 23/146.

Admission books for the years 1778-1756 and 1824-1917 are in WO 23/133, 163-172, 174-180. Arranged chronologically, these books give regiment, name, age, service, date of pension, cause of discharge, date of admission to pension, and decision of the Board of Chelsea Hospital. In addition, an address is often given. An index of in-pensioners admitted between 1858 and 1933 is in WO 23/173.

A list of in-pensioners at the Royal Hospital Kilmainham between 1839 and 1922 is in WO 118/47-48. This list also includes out-pensioners.

Pensions: other sources

Additional information about both in- and out- pensioners at Chelsea can sometimes be found in the Board Minutes and Papers, 1784-1953, in WO 250 and the Invaliding Board Minutes and Papers, 1800-1915, in WO 180, especially where appeals were made against decisions on eligibility for a pension and the rate at which it was to be paid Minute books in WO 180/53-76 include appeals as well as other relevant papers. The books are incomplete, and date from between 1823 and 1915.

A nominal list of out-pensioners discharged between 1821 and 1829, who had served in the tropics, for which an additional pension was payable, is in WO 23/25.

Some 5000 personal files of soldiers (and sailors) who received a disability pension and who left the armed services before 1914 are in PIN 71. A number of papers for widows' pensions are also included in this class. The files contain medical records, accounts of how and where illness or injuries occurred and men's own accounts of incidents in which they were involved. Conduct sheets are included, recording the place of birth, age, names of parents and family, religion, physical attributes and marital status.

7.8 Soldiers settling abroad

Pensions were also paid to former British soldiers who had emigrated to the colonies. Chelsea Hospital out-pension registers, 1814-1857, for these men are in WO 120/69-70. Another register, 1845-1854, is in WO 23/31.

Lists of men who emigrated to Australia and New Zealand between 1830 and 1848 under schemes to settle soldiers there are in WO 43/542 (for Australia) and WO 43/853 (New Zealand).

A more detailed description of the sources available is in Stella Colwell, *Family roots* (London, 1991).

7.9 Summary of records

To trace the service records of an individual it is important to know the approximate dates of his service and, if possible, the regiment or corps he served in.

The main series of personnel records are the attestation and discharge papers in WO 97. They survive for most men who did NOT die in service and who received a pension. Between 1750 and 1873 they are arranged by regiment. Relatively few of these records survive before 1792. The PRO holds none later than 1913. Further details of them are in section 7.2 above.

Pension papers are another source of information. They are in two series: WO 116 for medical pensions between 1715 and 1913, and WO 117 for service pensions between 1823 and 1913. For more information see section 7.7 . It is considerably more difficult to trace an ancestor who died in the Army. Muster rolls list each man in a regiment and are in WO 12. Further details are in section 7.4 above. If a man died during a campaign, especially in the late nineteenth century, he may be recorded on a casualty return. Details of casualty returns are in section 4.2 above.

8. ROYAL ARTILLERY

8.1 Introduction

The Royal Artillery was formed in 1716. The Royal Horse Artillery, which was originally part of it, was established in 1793. Until 1855 the Royal Artillery was under the control of the Ordnance Office rather than the War Office. As a result many of its records were kept separately and this separation is reflected in the current arrangement of the records, where much material relating to the Royal Artillery can be found in classes containing records relating to the Ordnance Office.

Marriage and birth registers for the Royal Artillery between 1817 and 1827, 1860 and 1877 are in WO 69/551-582.

8.2 Officers

A published *List of Officers of the Royal Regiment of Artillery*, 1716-June 1914 (3 vols, London 1899, 1914) is available in the Reference Room at Kew.

Records of service of officers, 1770-1902, are included in WO 76, for which there is an incomplete name index in the Reference Room at Kew. Earlier lists of officers, 1727-1751, are in WO 54/684, 701. Pay lists for officers, 1803-1871, are in WO 54/946. Other records include an incomplete series of commission books, 1740-1852, in WO 54/237-239, 244-247 and of officers for 1793 in WO 54/701. Original patents and warrants of appointment, 1670-1855, are in WO 54/939-945. Appointment papers for officers, 1809-1852, are in WO 54/917-922.

There are registers for officers receiving half pay between 1810 and 1880 in WO 23/82. For further details of half pay see section 6.7 above.

June's Woolwich Journal was a newspaper for the Royal Artillery at Woolwich. It contained news of officers, their movements with other interesting information. The PRO holds copies only for 1847 to 1850 in WO 62/48.

8.3 Other ranks

Records of service of soldiers in the Royal Artillery, 1791-1855, are in WO 69. They include attestation papers and show name, age, description, place of birth, trade, and dates of service, of promotions, of marriage and of discharge or death. These records are arranged under the unit in which the individual last served, which can be ascertained from indexes and posting books in WO 69/779-782, 801-839.

Soldiers' documents for the Royal Artillery between 1760 and 1854 are in WO 97, although there appear to be very few documents earlier than 1792.

Muster rolls for the Royal Artillery, 1708-1878, are in WO 10. Except for a few rolls, mostly for the eighteenth century, battalions which served in India are not included. Some later muster rolls are in WO 16. For an example, see figure 8 on page 72.

Entry books of discharges, transfers and casualties between 1740 and 1858 are in WO 54/317-328. Casualty returns from 1850 are in WO 25.

There is also an incomplete series of registers of deceased, discharged or deserted men, 1772-1774, 1816-1873, in WO 69/583-597, 644-647, arranged by artillery regiment. Description books for Royal Artillery battalions between 1749 and 1859 are in WO 54/260-309, and depots between 1773 and 1874 in WO 69/74-80. Books for the Royal Irish Artillery, 1756-1774, are in WO 69/620. A number of miscellaneous pay lists and other records of the Royal Artillery, 1692-1876, are in WO 54/672-755.

Registers of pensions, 1816-1833, are in WO 54/338-452, 470-480. Registers of pensions being paid in 1834, when responsibility for them was transferred from the Board of Ordnance to the Royal Hospital Chelsea, are in WO 23/141-145. In addition, there is in WO 116/127-185 a special series of admission books for Royal Artillery pensions between 1833 and 1913.

8.4 Royal Horse Artillery

Records of service of soldiers in the Royal Horse Artillery, 1803-1863, are in WO 69. Description books for the Royal Horse Artillery between 1776 and 1821 are in WO 69/1-6.

A number of application papers for posts in the Royal Horse Artillery between 1820 and 1851 are in WO 54/927. Baptism and marriage registers between 1859 and 1883 are in WO 69/63-73.

9. ROYAL ENGINEERS

9.1 Introduction

The Corps of Engineers, consisting of officers only, was established as part of the Board of Ordnance in 1717. It was given the Royal title in 1787. In the same year soldier-artificers, who worked under the engineer officers' supervision, were formed into the Corps of Royal Military Artificers. In 1806 junior officers were added to its establishment and in 1811 it became the Royal Corps of Sappers and Miners. The two Corps merged to form the Royal Engineers in 1856.

9.2 Officers

Engineer officers were until 1855 the responsibility not of the War Office but of the Board of Ordnance. Lists of engineer officers for 1793 are in WO 54/701. Registers of the establishment of the Royal Engineers for 1851 and 1855 are in WO 54/235-236. Commission books for officers, 1755-1852, are in WO 54/240-247. Returns of officers, showing stations where they were based between 1786 and 1850, are in WO 54/248-259. Appointment papers of officers, 1815-1846, are in WO 54/923-924. Pay lists for officers, 1805-1871, are in WO 54/947.

Records of service, 1796-1922, are in WO 25/3913-3919. These records include marriages and details of children of officers. An incomplete card index to these records is available in the Reference Room at Kew. Reports on students at the School of Military Engineering at Chatham, 1858-1914, are in WO 25/3945-3954. There are registers of officers receiving half pay between 1810 and 1880 in WO 23/82. For further details of half pay see section 6.7 above.

A list of officers has been published for the Royal Engineers called the *Roll of Officers of the Corps of Royal Engineers from 1660 to 1898* (London, 1898). A copy is available in the Reference Room at Kew.

Service records of officers who served in the Supply and Service Department of the Royal Engineers between 1828 and 1903 are in WO 25/3921-3922.

9.3 Other ranks

A register of deceased soldiers in both the Royal Engineers and the Royal Corps of Sappers and Miners, 1824-1858, is in WO 25/2972, and an abstract of effects and credits of deceased men for 1825 in WO 25/2973. Entry books of discharges, transfers and casualties for artificers, sappers and miners and Royal Engineers between 1800 and 1859 are in WO 54/329-335.

A return of sappers and miners entitled to pensions in 1830 is in WO 54/482. Registers of sapper and miner pensioners, compiled in 1834 but dating back to the Napoleonic Wars, are in WO 23/141-145. They include descriptions of individuals. Description books for sappers, miners and artificers, 1756-1833, are in WO 54/310-316.

Soldiers' documents for 1760 to 1854 are in WO 97/1148-1152, and from 1855 to 1872 in WO 97/1359-1364. For further information about soldiers' documents see section 7.2 above.

Muster rolls for the Royal Corps of Sappers and Miners and the Engineers between 1816 and 1878 are in WO 11. Further details about muster rolls are in section 7.4 above.

10. MILITIA AND VOLUNTEERS

10.1 Introduction

The militia had existed in various forms since Tudor times. Section 5.2 above describes the Tudor and Stuart militia and the records it created.

The Militia Act 1757 re-established one or more regiments for each county, raised from volunteers and conscripts chosen by ballot from each parish. Officers were appointed by the lord lieutenant of the county. In peacetime the militia assembled for drill and manoeuvres at intervals. After 1782 they came under the ultimate authority of the Home Secretary. In wartime, however, having been mobilized (or embodied) by royal proclamation, they were subject to the orders of the commander in chief and were liable to serve anywhere in the British Isles but not overseas.

The Fencible Infantry and Cavalry, which were regular regiments raised for home service only, are often classed with the militia.

Between 1804 and 1813 supplementary militia and volunteer units were raised. The men who served in them were not conscripts but were in other respects similar to the militia. In addition, however, they included cavalry regiments (the Yeomanry) and a proportion of artillery.

In 1859, as a result of local pressure and fears of a possible foreign invasion, volunteer regiments were again formed. They had little formal connection with the War Office until 1873. Thereafter, a small number of soldiers (including officers) or retired soldiers formed a permanent staff on each of these regiments.

After the reorganization of the Army on a territorial basis in 1881, the county militia regiments became the third battalions and the volunteer units the fourth and sometimes the fifth battalions of their local regiments. In 1908 the Militia was renamed the Special Reserve. The Volunteers and the Yeomanry (which later became the Territorial Force) were more closely integrated with it.

10.2 Officers

Information about appointment of officers to militia and volunteer units from 1782 to 1840 can be found in the Home Office Military Papers (HO 50), with related entry books in HO 51. The papers include some establishment and succession books, but there is no name index and in general no information is given beyond the names of officers and the dates of their commissions.

Records of service of officers in a number of militia regiments are in WO 68. They date from about 1757 to 1925, but are incomplete. Provided that the unit is known, it is possible to get a rough idea of an officer's service from the muster books in WO 13. Registers of pensions paid to militia officers, 1868-1892, are in WO 23/89-92. A selection of birth and baptismal certificates from 1788 to 1886 is in WO 32/8906-8913.

From 1865 names of officers appear in the Army List.

10.3 Other Ranks

The most useful records for the family historian are the attestation forms of those men who served in the militia, which are in WO 96. They range in date from 1806 to 1915, but the majority are from the second half of the nineteenth century. They are arranged alphabetically by surname order under the name of the regular regiment to which the militia unit was attached. In form and content they are similar to soldiers' documents, which are described in section 7.2 above.

Muster books and pay lists of the English, Scottish, Irish and Colonial Militia, and the Fencible Infantry and Cavalry, Yeomanry, Irish Yeomanry and Volunteers from 1780 to 1878 are in WO 13. Muster books and pay lists provide a means of establishing the dates of enlistment and discharge or death. When an individual appears for the first time the entry in the muster book may show his age. For volunteer units only, payments to the professional cadre, and not the ordinary volunteers, are included.

Muster books are of use only if you know which unit your ancestor belonged to. Records of payments to the families of those men who served in militia units during the Napoleonic Wars are in E 182 at Chancery Lane. A number of soldiers' documents for men who served in militia regiments between 1760 and 1854 are in WO 97/1091-1112. They are arranged in name order, and appear to be mainly for Irish regiments. Very few of them date from before 1792. A list of Chelsea pensioners discharged from militia and yeomanry regiments between 1821 and 1829 is in WO 23/25.

10.4 Further information

The vast majority of other militia records are in WO 68. They include order books, succession books, records of officers' services and enrolment books. A number of muster books for units based in London and Middlesex are in WO 70. Records for a few provincial units are in WO 79. Records of the Tower Hamlets Militia are in WO 94.

Many records of militia and volunteer units are preserved at local record offices. These records are described in Jeremy Gibson and Mervyn Medlycott, *Militia lists and musters, 1757-1876* (FFHS, 1990). For further details of record offices see appendix 4 below.

11. MEDALS AND AWARDS, 1793-1913

11.1 Introduction

Medals in their present form are a nineteenth century innovation. During the eighteenth century special medals in gold or silver were sometimes struck to commemorate great victories, but they were privately minted and given only to senior officers. There are three types of medal: campaign, gallantry, and long service and good conduct. Some files about the creation and design of these medals are in MINT 16. A full account of the award of British medals is given in E C John, A R Litherland and B T Simpkin, *British Battles and Medals* (London, 1988), a copy of which is available in the Reference Room at Kew.

11.2 Campaign medals

Campaign medals were issued to all men who had served in a particular campaign or battle or who had completed a certain number of years meritorious service. The first campaign medal awarded by the British government was the Waterloo Medal. The Waterloo Medal Book, in MINT 16/112, records the corps and regiments engaged in the battle, giving the name and rank of officers and men. This medal proved so popular that medals were subsequently awarded for most major campaigns. General service medals were also issued, to which bars or clasps could be added for specific battles or for minor campaigns. The first of these was the Military General

Service Medal issued for service in North America and the Peninsular War (1793-1814). Men who received this medal are listed in K D N Kingsley-Foster, *Military General Service Medal, 1793-1814* (London, 1947) and Capt Lionel S Challis, *Peninsular Roll Call* (London, 1948). Copies of both books are available in the Reference Room at Kew.

Awards of campaign medals are recorded on medal rolls in WO 100. They are arranged first by regiment, then rank, then name. For an example see figure 12 on page 76. For most medals the only information given is the recipient's number and a note of the bars to which he was entitled. Both the Queen's South Africa Medal and the King's South Africa Medal rolls, however, do give more information about the service of individuals. In addition, there are various files dealing with recommendations for awards, mainly for small colonial campaigns:

Campaign	Reference
Kurdistan (1925)	WO 32/3564
New Zealand (1861, 1863)	WO 32/8258, 8270
Nubia, Sudan (1926-1927)	WO 32/3537
Rhodesia (1898)	WO 32/7840, 7842-7843
Sierra Leone (1898)	WO 32/7629, 7632, 7635
Somaliland (1903-1904)	WO 32/8428, 8440
South Africa (1878-1879)	WO 32/7682, 7764
South Africa (1899-1903)	WO 32/7960, WO 108/136-179
Sudan (1884-1886, 1896-1898)	WO 32/3539
Tsingtao, China (1914-1915)	WO 32/4996B

Campaign medal rolls for the First World War are in WO 329. Further details of these records are in section 17.4 below.

11.3   Long service and good conduct medals

In 1833 a Long Service and Good Conduct Medal was instituted for soldiers who had served eighteen years in the Army. Medal rolls for this medal between 1831 and 1953 are in WO 102. Awards of long service medals to officers in colonial forces, 1891-1894, are in WO 32/8293-8298. WO 102 also contains some rolls for medals issued to men serving in militia and colonial forces.

In 1846 a Meritorious Service Medal was authorized for sergeants and warrant officers who had performed good service other than in battle. Awards for meritorious service between 1846 and 1919 are in WO 101. A register of annuities paid to recipients of the meritorious or long service awards, 1846-1879, is in WO 23/84. Rolls for the Volunteer Officers' Decoration, 1892-1932, are in WO 330.

11.4   Gallantry medals

Gallantry medals were awarded for a specific act of heroism.

The Distinguished Conduct Medal was established in December 1854 to reward other anks for distinguished service in the Crimea. In 1856 the Victoria Cross was instituted and the first awards were announced in the *London Gazette* of 24 February 1857 for heroes of the Crimean War. It quickly became the most coveted of all British gallantry medals.

The Victoria Cross remained the only medal for gallantry which could be awarded to officers until the Distinguished Service Order was instituted in 1886, although the CB (Companion of the Bath) was frequently given to field officers for distinguished services.

Citations for gallantry medals, especially for the period leading up to and including the First World War, are in the *London Gazette*, copies of which are held at the PRO in ZJ 1.

Submissions to the Sovereign for the award of the Distinguished Conduct Medal are in WO 146 and often contain citations. A few files about the award of this medal to individuals are in WO 32 (code 50S). Individual recipients are listed in P E Abbott, *Recipients of the Distinguished Conduct Medal, 1855-1909* (London, 1975). Registers of the award of the Victoria Cross and submissions to the Sovereign, 1856-1953, are in WO 98. For an example see figure 13 on page 77. A list of recipients of the medal, 1856-1946, is in CAB 106/320. Files about the award of the medal to individuals between 1856 and 1957 are in WO 32 (code 50M). Citations for the Victoria Cross during the Second World War are in CAB 106/312. Registers of the award of the CB, 1815-1894, are in WO 104. Files about the award of the Distinguished Service Order, 1886-1908, are in WO 32 (code 52C).

11.5 Mentions in Despatches

Medals were not the only honour available. A man could be mentioned in despatches. This was one of the oldest ways of recognizing meritorious service or gallant behaviour. In reports after battles and campaigns, commanding generals would single out those who had been brought to their attention, sometimes merely listing their names, but occasionally including a brief description of their services. Before 1843 only officers were mentioned. There was no distinctive decoration or even a certificate for those singled out, but the names were published in the *London Gazette* and, for officers, mentions in despatches were listed in the Army List.

A few files about individuals who were mentioned in despatches are in WO 32 (code 51). A list of people mentioned in despatches during the South African War, 1901, is in WO 108/142.

12. COURTS MARTIAL

12.1 Introduction

There were three different types of court martial for which the PRO holds records: general courts martial, general regimental courts martial (before 1829) and district courts martial (after 1829).

12.2 Officers

Tracing the courts martial of commissioned officers is relatively straightforward, since they could be tried only by general court martial. WO 93/1B is an index to trials of officers, 1806-1904. WO 93/1A is an index to general courts martial between 1806 and 1833.

There are three main types of record relating to individual trials: papers, proceedings and registers. Papers were compiled at the time of the court martial and are arranged in date order. They are in WO 71/121-343 and cover the period between 1688 and 1850, with one file for 1879. Other papers for trials between 1850 and 1914 were destroyed by enemy bombing in 1940. Papers for some special cases, mainly senior officers, are listed individually between 1780 and 1824 in WO 71/99-120, as are special returns for Ireland, 1800-1820, which are in WO 71/252-264.

When papers reached the Judge Advocate General's Office, their contents were entered into the volumes of proceedings. They were kept in two series depending on whether the sentence was confirmed at home by the Sovereign, or abroad by a colonial governor or overseas commander. These records are in WO 71/13-98 and continued in WO 91. Until the mid-nineteenth century, the proceedings report the trials in detail, but later volumes give only the charges, findings and sentences in the form in which they were handed to the Sovereign. They also contain copies of warrants for the holding of courts martial and correspondence concerning the confirmation of sentences. Registers of warrants are in WO 28. The commander in chief's submissions upon sentence are in WO 209.

As well as volumes of proceedings, the Judge Advocate General's Office compiled registers of courts martial, giving the name, rank, regiment, place of trial, charge, finding and sentence. Registers of courts martial confirmed abroad are in WO 90 and those confirmed at home are in WO 92. Records of field general courts martial date only from the South African War (1899-1902) and are combined in registers with district courts martial, for 1900 and 1901 only, in WO 92. Later registers, between 1909 and 1963, are in WO 213.

12.3 Other ranks

NCOs and ordinary soldiers could be tried by general regimental courts martial (before 1829) and district courts martial (after 1829), as well as by general courts martial. As a result it is more difficult to find the records of individual cases. Only registers, rather than full proceedings, were compiled in the Judge Advocate General's Office. Registers of general regimental courts martial, between 1812 and 1829, are in WO 89 and of district courts martial, between 1829 and 1971, in WO 86. Both classes contain trials confirmed both at home and abroad, except those for London, 1865-1875, which are in WO 87, and India, 1878-1945, in WO 88.

For general courts martial the records are as described for officers above.

12.4 Other sources

Records relating to individual cases are closed for 75 years from the date of the last entry in each piece. However, purely summary records of a more recent date are open. WO 93/40 gives particulars of death sentences carried out between 1941 and 1953. Nominal rolls of courts martial of all ranks of Australian and Canadian forces, 1915-1919, are in WO 93/42-45. A list of death sentences carried out in the British Army during the First World War is in WO 93/49. Nominal rolls of courts held in the Prisoners of War camp at Changi, 1942-1944, are in WO 93/46-48. Statistics for army and air force courts martial, 1914-1954, are in WO 93/49-59.

13. THE BRITISH ARMY IN INDIA AND THE INDIAN ARMY

13.1 Introduction

Until 1859 the army in India belonged to the East India Company and consisted of separate regiments of European and Indian troops led by European officers. After 1859, the European regiments became part of the British Army and the Indian troops became the Indian Army under the control of the viceroy in Delhi.

Service records for officers and soldiers of the East India Company army and its successors are, for the most part, held by the British Library, Oriental and India Office Collections. These records include registers of births, marriages and deaths. The Library also holds entry papers for officer cadets between 1789 and 1860. These papers include baptismal certificates and educational qualifications. Also kept by the Library are registers of recruits, 1817-1860, and embarkation lists, 1753-1861. A brief description of the records held by the British Library is in appendix 4 below.

13.2 East India Company and Indian Army

A few records relating to the East India Company and Indian Army are held by the PRO. Lists of officers of the European regiments, 1796-1841, are in WO 25/3215-3219.

Registers of service of every officer holding a commission on 1 November 1871 are in the papers of the Army Purchase Commission in WO 74, together with a series of applications from officers on Indian establishments, 1871-1891, to which certificates of service are attached. Papers and applications are indexed by regiment but not by name of applicant.

Registers and indexes of East India Company Army pensions, 1849-1876, and Indian Army pensions, 1849-1868, are in WO 23/17-23. A register of pensions paid to former soldiers serving with the East India Company between 1824 and 1856 is in WO 25/3137. Lists of deserters from the Company's army between 1844 and 1851 are in WO 25/2933.

War diaries of Indian Army formations during the First World War are in WO 95. War diaries for the Second World War are in WO 169-WO 179.

13.3   British Army in India

Service Records of officers and men generally, for the British Army in India as for all others, are described in sections 6 and 7 above.

A list of British officers who served in India between 1796 and 1804 is in WO 25/3215. Records for soldiers discharged on return from India before 1806 will be found in the depot musters of their regiments. Between 1863 and 1878 the discharges of men returning from India are recorded in the musters of the Victoria Hospital, Netley (WO 12/13077-13105); between 1862 and 1889 similar information is in the muster rolls of the Discharge Depot at Gosport (WO 16/2284, 2888-2915). Except for a few eighteenth century Artillery rolls, there are no musters of artillery and engineers in India but musters of infantry and cavalry regiments in India between 1883 and 1889 are in WO 16/2751-2887.

13.4   Other sources

Registers of the deaths of officers in all the Indian services for the Second World War are held by the British Library, Oriental and India Office Collections. Registers of garrison churches, and other churches used by soldiers and their families, are held by the diocesan authorities in India. Births, marriages and deaths for officers and men of the British Army in India appear in the Chaplain's Returns held at St Catherine's House. Details of these records are given in appendix 4 below.

The National Army Museum holds Hodson's Index, a very large card index of British Officers in the Indian Army, the Bengal Army and the East India Company Army, but not the British Army in India. Many of the entries go beyond bare facts to include colourful stories of life. Civilians and government staff are included if they had seen army life. Details of the holdings of the National Army Museum are given in appendix 4 below.

Two useful books are V C P Hodgson, *Lists of Officers of the Bengal Army* (London, 1927-1928, revised 1968) and Byron Farwell, *Armies of the Raj* (London, 1990) which is a social history of the Indian Army.

14. COLONIAL AND DOMINIONS FORCES

14.1 Introduction, 1754-1902

Soldiers' documents for men who served in colonial regiments between 1760 and 1872 are in WO 97. Microfilmed copies of these records for regiments raised, or primarily serving, in Canada are held by the National Archives of Canada, 395 Wellington Street, Ottawa, K1A 0N3 Canada.

Muster books of certain colonial regiments are in WO 12 and those of colonial militia are in WO 13. Many men from the colonies, especially those of Canadian origin, served with the 100th Foot.

Half pay returns for officers who had served in Canadian forces between 1783 and 1813 are in WO 24/748-762.

Returns of NCOs and men serving with colonial units in 1806 are in WO 25/1070-1121.

Admission books for pensions payable in the colonies, 1817-1875, are in WO 23/147-152. There is an admission book for native and colonial pensioners, 1880-1903, in WO 23/160. Other registers of pensions paid to colonial soldiers are in WO 22.

Casualty lists for colonial regiments between 1797 and 1817 are in WO 25/1345-1357, 2183-2207, 2242-2295, with indexes in WO 25/2689-2713, 2734-2753. Further indexes to casualty returns, 1850 to 1910, are in WO 25/3465-3471.

The National Archives of Canada has a number of records relating to British and Canadian militia forces stationed in the country. These records are summarised in *Tracing your ancestors in Canada* (1991). This pamphlet is available free of charge from the National Archives.

14.2 Records of individual colonial regiments

There are description books for officers in the following regiments:

Unit	Date	Reference
Cape Mounted Rifles	1825-1865	WO 25/636-637
Ceylon Rifles	1809-1872	WO 25/638-641
Royal African Corps	1808-1815	WO 25/626
Royal Canadian Rifles	1841-1868	WO 25/632-633
West India Rangers	1804-1816	WO 25/663
West India Regiments	1826-1869	WO 25/646-650 652, 660

In addition, returns of officers' services compiled in 1829 and 1872 for a number of regiments are in WO 25/805, 824, 840, 854 and 869. Further details about these records are in section 6.6 above.

Lists, registers and admission books for negro and Cape Mounted Rifle Corps pensioners, 1837-1879, are in WO 23/153-157, 159. Another admission book for men serving in the Ceylon Regiment and the Gun Lascars between 1868 and 1876 is in WO 23/158.

Lists of soldiers employed by the Royal African Company between 1756 and 1815 are in T 70/1454-1456. The papers of the Company (in T 70) contain a great deal of information about garrisons in West Africa.

14.3 North America, 1746-1783

Lists of men who served in certain provincial volunteer forces in North America, 1746-1747, 1775-1783, are in WO 28/1, 4-5. Further muster rolls for militia units in the colonies of Connecticut, Massachusetts, New Hampshire and Rhode Island between 1759 and 1763 are in T 64/22. A list of officers who served in provincial forces during the American War of Independence is in T 64/23. Certificates of birth, baptism, marriage and death for a number of officers in Loyal American and Canadian units between 1776 and 1881 are in WO 42/59-63. Lists of men who served with the North and South Carolina militia are in T 50.

Some muster rolls of provincial loyalist troops in the American War of Independence are preserved in the National Archives of Canada, 395 Wellington Street, Ottawa, K1A 0N3 Canada.

14.4 South Africa, 1899-1902

Service records and attestation papers for men who served in locally recruited volunteer forces during the South African War (1899-1902) are in WO 126 and WO 127. Soldiers' documents for the Imperial Yeomanry are in WO 128. They are arranged by regimental number which may be found in the indexes in WO 129/1-7. Casualties are recorded in WO 129/8-11 and WO 108/338. Details are also available in *South African Field Force Casualty List, 1899-1902* (London, 1972) which is available in the Reference Room at Kew.

Records relating to Canadian troops who fought in the war are held by the National Archives of Canada.

Records of men who served in Natal volunteer regiments or the militia between 1884 and 1912 are held by the Natal Archives Depot, Private Bag, X9012, 3200 Pietermaritzburg South Africa.

14.5 1902-1953

Records relating to members of colonial and dominion forces can sometimes be found among relevant records of the Colonial and Dominions Offices. Original correspondence relating to the King's African Rifles, which was formed in 1902 from the armed forces of various East African dependencies, is in CO 534, with registers in CO 623 and CO 624. Original correspondence for the Niger and West Africa Force, formed in 1897, is in CO 445, with registers in CO 581 and CO 582. From 1927 correspondence about various colonial forces is in CO 820.

War diaries of colonial and dominion forces for the First World War are in WO 95. Casualty records and medal rolls for Canadian forces in the South African and First World Wars are held by the Canadian Department of Veteran Affairs, Honours and Awards, 284 Wellington Street, Ottawa, K1A 0P4, Canada.

War diaries for colonial forces for the Second World War are in WO 169-WO 178. With the exception of Australia and Southern Rhodesia, war diaries for forces of the dominions are in WO 179. War diaries for Southern Rhodesian Forces are in WO 333. Australian war diaries are held by the Australian War Memorial, GPO Box 345, Canberra, ACT 2601 Australia.

CO 820/50/1-12 contain nominal rolls for British and European officers and other ranks serving with local forces in certain non-African colonies.

During the Korean War (1950-1953), the Commonwealth Division included several Australian and Canadian units. The war diaries for all these units are in WO 281. Service records for men who served in the Australian armed forces after 1914 are held by the Historical Research Centre, Central Army Records Office, 360 St Kilda Road, Melbourne, VIC 3044 Australia. An extensive collection of material relating to all branches of the Australian fighting services is held by the Australian War Memorial, GPO Box 345, Canberra, ACT 2601 Australia. The War Memorial is unable to undertake genealogical research, but will suggest professional researchers to do the work for you. Their holdings are described in Joyce Bradley et al, *Roll call! A guide to genealogical sources in the Australian War Memorial* (Canberra, 1986).

Service records for Canadians who served during the two world wars are held by the Personnel Records Centre, National Archives of Canada, Tunney's Pasture, Ottawa, K1A 0N3 Canada.

Naval, army and air force service records for New Zealanders between 1899 and 1979 are held by Base Records, Ministry of Defence, Private Bag, Wellington, New Zealand. Records held by the National Archives of New Zealand, PO Box 6148, Te Aro, Wellington include nineteenth century material relating to British imperial troops, pensioner settlers, local militia and volunteer corps military settlers of the 1860s. More recent records include material on conscription, reservists and war diaries. These records are described in more detail in *Family History at the National Archives* (Wellington, NZ, 1990).

Service records for South African servicemen from 1912 are held by the Military Information Bureau, Archives Section, Private Bag X289, 0001 Pretoria, South Africa. The Bureau will do searches for family historians. The National Archives of South Africa, Private Bag X206, 0001 Pretoria hold some military records. Of particular interest are the personal files of the South African Constabulary which many British soldiers joined at the end of the South African War (1899-1902), usually for a short time before returning to England or going to another colony. These records are described in more detail in R T J Lombard, *Handbook for Genealogical Research in South Africa* (Pretoria, 1990).

The Commonwealth Forces History Trust, 37 Davis Road, London W3 7SE, may be able to help people interested in the history or records of colonial and dominion army units.

15. FOREIGN TROOPS IN BRITISH PAY

15.1 Introduction

Many of the records described elsewhere in this handbook include information about foreign troops in British pay. In particular many foreigners, especially Germans, served with the 60th Foot.

15.2 1775-1816

Muster rolls of Hessian troops in British pay in North America, 1776-1794 and 1796-1797, are in AO 3/55, 58-59. Pay lists between 1775 and 1795 are in T 38/812-814. An index of names is available in the Reference Room at Kew. Further information about these Hessian soldiers may be obtained from the Institut fuer Archivwissenschaft, Archivschule Marburg, D-3550 Marburg an der Lahn, Germany.

Muster rolls of French royalist forces in British pay during the Napoleonic Wars are amongst the Bouillon papers in HO 69. Musters and pay lists for officers in the French Emigrant Engineers and Artillery are in WO 54/702.

Some birth, baptism, marriage and death certificates for officers in French, Greek, Swiss and Italian Corps are in WO 42/64-65. They cover the period between 1776 and 1881, but are mostly for the Napoleonic Wars.

Statements were taken in June 1806 of the period of service of all NCOs and men in certain French refugee units. Those for the Chasseurs Britanniques are in WO 25/1099 and for Dillon's and Meuron's Regiments in WO 25/1116-1117. A list of men discharged from foreign regiments between 1783 and 1810 is in WO 25/1121.

Casualty returns for foreign troops between 1809 and 1816 are in WO 25/2267-2271, 2289-2292, with indexes in WO 25/2753, 2892. Muster rolls of foreign regiments are in WO 12. Those for units of foreign artillery are in WO 10.

Histories of foreign regiments in the British army, 1793-1802, are given in the *Journal of the Society for Army Historical Research* vol 22 (1943-1944).

15.3 King's German Legion

Soon after the resumption of the Napoleonic Wars in 1803 attempts were made to recruit foreign troops to serve in the British Army. The Hanoverian army had been disbanded under the terms of the Treaty of Amiens, and special efforts were made by the British to recruit former members of this army. Virtually all members of the King's German Legion came from Hanover.

The Legion fought in the Baltic, in Spain, and in Southern France. In 1815 it took part in the Battle of Waterloo. It was disbanded in 1816 and many of the officers and men joined the reformed Hanoverian army.

Former officers of the Legion were asked to supply details of their service in 1828. These records, arranged alphabetically, are in WO 25/749-779. There is an incomplete card index, arranged by name, in the Reference Room at Kew. Some birth, baptism, marriage and death certificates for officers are to be found in WO 42/52-58.

Soldiers' documents for men who served in the Legion are in WO 97/1178-1181. A register of recruits for the Legion, 1803-1808, is in WO 25/3203. Statements taken in June 1806 of the period of service of all NCOs and men serving with the Legion are in WO 25/1100-1114. A list of men discharged from the Legion between 1783 and 1810 is in WO 25/1121.

Casualty returns for the Legion are in WO 25/2272-2288, with indexes in WO 25/

2752, 2888-2891. Muster rolls are in WO 12/11747-11948. Muster rolls for artillery units attached to the Legion are in WO 10. Lists of all the men of the Legion present at the Battle of Waterloo are in WO 12/11949. An index to names is available in the Reference Room at Kew.

A register of pensioners from the Legion, 1801-1815, is in WO 23/135. Lists of men discharged to pension in 1816 are in WO 25/3236-3237 and WO 116/25. They give the reason for discharge, age, and place of birth of individuals. An alphabetical list of men in these volumes is kept at the Reference Room desk at Kew. Registers of payments made between 1843 and 1867 to soldiers who had served in the Legion are in PMG 7. Many records of the Legion are held by the Niedersaechsischen Hauptstaatarchiv, Am Archiv 1, D-3000 Hannover 1, Germany.

15.4 1815-1854

Discharge documents for men who served in the Foreign Veterans Battalion, 1815-1861, are in WO 122, together with reports of medical boards on individuals in these regiments, 1816-1817. A statement of the service by officers in foreign legions from about 1817 is in WO 25/3236-3237.

Registers of half pay given to officers who had served with foreign regiments, 1819-1824, are in WO 24/763-766. Other registers of half pay and pensions to former officers who had served in foreign regiments between 1822 and 1885 are in PMG 6.

15.5 The Crimean War

At the outbreak of the War in 1854 foreign mercenary troops were recruited for service in the Crimea. They formed the British German, Swiss, and Italian Legions. Muster rolls, service records and attestation forms for the British German and Swiss Legions are in WO 15 (none have survived for the Italian Legion). At the end of the War the Legions were disbanded and many men emigrated to the Cape of Good Hope. WO 15 also contains a list of officers and men of the British German Legion who settled in the Cape in 1856. The families who emigrated are listed in Esme Bull, *Aided immigration from Britain to South Africa, 1857-1867* (Pretoria, 1990).

Returns of half pay made to officers of foreign regiments between 1858 and 1876 are in WO 23/79-81. Registers of payments to widows of officers between 1855 and 1858 are in WO 23/113, and between 1858 and 1868 in WO 23/88.

Further information is given in C C Bayley, *Mercenaries for the Crimea* (London, 1977).

15.6 Second World War

A number of Polish soldiers escaped after the collapse of Poland in 1939 and fought in Polish units attached to allied armies during the war. War diaries for some Polish units are in WO 169 and WO 170.

Because of the political situation in Poland many of these soldiers and their families did not wish to return home after the war had ended. A Polish Resettlement Corps was set up in 1946 to ease the transition of Poles to civilian life in Britain and abroad. The records of the Corps are in WO 315 and contain many items of interest to the family historian. A number of the files are in Polish, however, and some have either been retained by the Ministry of Defence or are closed for 75 years.

Service records of Free Poles are retained by the Ministry of Defence, CS (Records) Polish Branch, Bourne Avenue, Hayes, Middx UB3 1RF. MoD will undertake a search only on receipt of a written request from the next of kin.

16. RECORDS OF ANCILLARY SERVICES

16.1 Barrackmasters

Barrackmasters were responsible for the construction and maintenance of barracks. A separate Barrackmaster General's Department was established under War Office control in 1792. In 1808 the department was transferred to the Treasury, and then in 1822 to the Board of Ordnance. On the transfer of the Board to the War Office in 1855 the department was disbanded.

Barrackmasters are listed in the monthly Army Lists. WO 54 includes appointment papers and testimonials for barrackmasters between 1808 and 1852, and for barrackmaster sergeants, 1823-1855 (WO 54/715-716, 756-823, 928-929). Some papers about the appointment of barrackmasters and their staff between 1835 and 1879 also appear in the registers of the Commissariat Department in WO 61/7-11. Pay and allowance books, 1797-1824, are in WO 54/704-713. Returns of service of barrackmasters in the British Isles, 1830-1852, are in WO 54/734, 742. An alphabetical list of barrackmaster sergeants, 1771-1824, is in WO 54/948.

16.2 Chaplains

Until the end of the eighteenth century chaplains were employed on a regimental and garrison basis. In 1796 a chaplain general was appointed and chaplains were allocated, one to a brigade or to three or four regiments. The first Presbyterian chaplains were appointed in 1827, Roman Catholics in 1836, Wesleyans in 1881, and Jewish chaplains in 1892.

Registers of certificates of service of chaplains, 1817-1843, are in WO 25/256-258. Lists of payments to chaplains, 1805-1842, are in WO 25/233-251, 254-255. Lists of chaplains receiving retired pay, 1806-1837, are in WO 25/252-253. Information about the appointment of chaplains and their conditions of pay and service is in the out-letter books of the War Office Accounts Department, 1810-1836, in WO 7/60-65, and in the in-letters of the Chaplain General's Department, 1808-1828, in WO 7/66-72.

Short biographies of chaplains are in *Crockford's Clerical Directory* and the *Catholic*

Directory. Chaplains are British army officers and so are included in the Army Lists. Further records are held by Ministry of Defence Chaplains, Bagshot Park, Bagshot GU19 5PL.

16.3   Civilian employees

Many thousands of men in dozens of different occupations have always been employed to help run the Army. Unfortunately very few records of their employment have survived. Senior civil servants at the War Office are listed in the *Imperial Calendar* and the *War Office List* published between 1861 and 1964. The List often includes brief biographies of certain individuals. It is available in the Reference Room at Kew.

Registers of pensions and superannuation payable to civilian employees, 1820-1892, are in WO 23/93-104. Pay books, rolls of names and other papers for civilians employed by the War Office between 1803 and 1919 are in WO 25/3957-3991.

Records of the War Office Boy Messenger Friendly Society and War Office School are in WO 371 and WO 32. The Society was set up in 1906 and continued until the outbreak of the First World War in 1914: a list of its members is in WO 371/3.

16.4   Commissariat

The Commissariat Department was responsible for the victualling of the Army and was set up in 1793. In 1816 the Department came under the control of the Treasury, but was transferred back to the War Office in 1854. Commissary officers were normally civilians but were subject to military discipline and wore uniform.

There are registers of full pay, half pay and pensions awarded to Commissary Officers between 1810 and 1856 in WO 61/61-93, with lists of pensions granted to widows, 1814-1826, in WO 61/96-97. Registers of half pay awarded to officers between 1834 and 1885 are in PMG 5.

Description and succession books for officers between 1855 and 1869, especially those in the Military Train (which was responsible for supplying the Army while abroad), are in WO 25/580-602, 824. Returns of officers' services for the Military Train in 1868 and 1869 are in WO 25/824/2.

Registers in WO 61/1-16 cover the appointment of men to the department between 1798 and 1889. Establishment lists, in WO 61/25-60, give the names of men employed in Spain and Portugal in 1809, and at various stations at home and abroad between 1816 and 1868.

Applications for employment as clerks in the Commissariat, 1812-1813, 1825-1854 are in WO 61/104-105. Letters relating to civilian appointments in the Commissariat, 1798-1855, are in WO 58/1-47. Registers of appointments and other papers relating to the employment of civil staff by the Commissariat, 1789-1879, are in WO 61.

16.5   Invalids and Veterans

From the late seventeenth century a number of companies of invalids were formed.

They consisted of soldiers partly disabled by wounds, and veterans who, from old age and length of service, had been rendered incapable of the duties of an active campaign, but were able to undertake lighter duties. Invalid companies were engaged in garrison duty both at home and in the colonies. The first companies were raised in 1690. From 1703 responsibility for raising and administering the companies was placed with the Royal Hospital Chelsea, and a Royal Corps of Invalids was formed. In 1804 the Royal Corps was disbanded. Invalids fit for service became part of the new Royal Garrison Regiment, the remainder went on to the strength of the newly formed Veteran Battalions. These battalions were used extensively to maintain civil peace at home until 1843, when they were re-formed as the Enrolled Pensioners. In 1867 the Pensioners were merged into the Second Class Army Reserve available for home service.

Description and succession books for officers serving with the Garrison Battalions between 1809 and 1815 are in WO 25/567, 571-573, 578. Other description books for Veteran Battalions between 1813 and 1826 are in WO 25/605-625. Records of officers serving with the Royal Garrison Regiment between 1901 and 1905 are in WO 19.

Soldiers' documents for men serving in Veteran Battalions between 1804 and 1854 are in WO 97. A register of men in the Garrison and Veteran Battalions, 1845-1854, is in WO 23/27. There is a series of certificates of service in Invalid and Veteran Battalions, 1782-1833, in WO 121/137-222.

Casualty returns for both the Veteran and Garrison regiments, 1809-1830, are in WO 25 2190-2195, 2216-2243.

Muster returns for companies and battalions are in WO 12. Monthly returns for companies stationed at garrisons, 1759 to 1802, which sometimes include lists of officers, are in WO 17/793-802.

A brief history of the invalids may be found in Michael Mann, 'The Corps of Invalids', *Journal of the Society for Army Historical Research* vol 66, no 1 (1988).

16.6   Medical services

Before 1855 medical services in the Army were provided on a regimental basis under the supervision of, from 1810, the Army Medical Department. In 1855 NCOs and men serving in hospitals were formed into the Medical Staff Corps, from 1857 the Army Hospital Corps. The regimental system was abolished in 1873 and all medical officers became part of a common Army Medical Department staff. In September 1884 the Department and the Army Hospital Corps were linked together in close association, and they finally merged to form the Royal Army Medical Corps in 1898.

Returns of medical staff in Great Britain, 1811-1813, are in WO 25/259-260, with returns of pay, 1813-1818, at home, in the Peninsula and in France in WO 25/261-263. Pay lists for Staff medical officers, clerks and apothecaries, 1799-1847, and regimental surgeons and assistants, 1790-1847, are in WO 25/3897-3902, with an index in WO 25/3903.

Service records for officers of the Medical Department between 1800 and 1840 are in WO 25/3904-3911, with an index in WO 25/3912. They include details of medical education received. Indexed volumes of candidates for commission as surgeons, 1825-1867, are in WO 25/3923-3943. Confidential reports on medical officers in 1860 and 1861 are in WO 25/3944.

A published *List of Commissioned Medical Officers of the Army, 1660-1960* (2 vols, 1925, 1968) is available in the Reference Room at Kew.

Soldiers' documents for the Army Hospital Corps, 1855-1872, are in WO 97/1698. The Royal Army Medical Corps medal book, 1879-1896, is in WO 25/3992.

Appointment papers for the Ordnance Board Medical Department, 1835-1847, are in WO 54/926. Returns of officers and men serving with the department between 1835 and 1850 are in WO 54/234 and 926.

16.7 Nursing services

Florence Nightingale's hospital at Scutari during the Crimean War (1854-1856) was the first to use women as nurses for British soldiers. Prior to this nursing duties were carried out by male orderlies seconded by regiments to serve in regimental hospitals. Six women nurses and a superintendent were employed by the Army Hospital Corps to serve at Woolwich and Netley in 1861. An Army Nursing Service was formed in 1881 and efforts were made to increase the numbers of female nurses in the Army. An Army Nursing Reserve was established in 1897. Both the Reserve and the Service were reorganized after the South African War (1899-1902) as Queen Alexandra's Imperial Military Nursing Service (QAIMNS). The present title of Queen Alexandra's Royal Army Nursing Corps (QARANC) was assumed in 1949.

The PRO holds no service records for members of the Army Nursing Service and its successors, although there are other records which might help in tracing the career of a nurse in the Army.

Testimonials for nurses who wished to serve with Florence Nightingale during the Crimean War are in WO 25/264. For an example see figure 14 on page 78. Nominal and seniority rolls for nurses in the voluntary National Aid Society and the Army Nursing Service, 1869-1891, are in WO 25/3955. An indexed register of candidates for appointment as staff nurses, 1903-1926, is in WO 25/3956.

An incomplete roll of nurses who served with the QAIMNS is in WO 162/16. Pension records prior to 1905 are in WO 23/93-95, 181. Few nurses qualified for a pension, however, because they rarely served enough years to receive one. Registers of pensions for nurses, 1909-1928, are in PMG 34/1-5.

In 1883 Queen Victoria instituted the Royal Red Cross to be awarded to military nurses. A register for its award from 1883 to 1918 is in WO 145. The Queen's and King's South Africa Medals were awarded to nurses for service during the South African War, 1899-1902; medal rolls are in WO 100.

Awards of medals to nurses during the First World War are in the medal rolls in WO 329. There is a separate name index to nurses on microfiche in the Microfilm Reading Room at Kew.

No service records for nurses in QAIMNS for the First World War are known to survive, but some records for nurses with the Territorial Nursing Service are held by the

Ministry of Defence. They also hold some service records for the Second World War. For further details see section 17.2 below.

Record cards for Voluntary Aid Detachment (VAD) nurses during both world wars are held by the British Red Cross Society, Archive Section, Bamett Hill, Wonersh, Guildford, Surrey, GU5 0RF.

Further information is contained in PRO Records Information Leaflet 120, *Military nurses and nursing services: record sources in the Public Record Office.*

16.8   Ordnance Office

The Ordnance Office was run separately from the War Office until 1855. It was responsible for the supply of guns, ammunition and warlike stores to the Army. It also controlled the Royal Artillery and the Royal Engineers. A brief administrative history of the Office is in the *Current Guide* Part 1, section 705. Records relating to the Royal Engineers and the Royal Artillery are described in sections 8 and 9 above.

Registers of employees of the Board of Ordnance, 1871-1847, are in WO 54/511-671. Appointment papers for barrackmasters, clerks and other people employed by the Board between 1819 and 1855 are in WO 54/756-903, 927.

Miscellaneous correspondence relating to people employed by the Office is in WO 44/695-700.

Registers of Ordnance pensions being paid in 1834, when responsibility was transferred to the Royal Hospital Chelsea, are in WO 23/141-145.

The monthly Orders of the Army Ordnance Corps, 1901-1919, are in WO 111. These include a great deal about promotions, awards, deaths, discharges and courts martial. Further information on the Ordnance Office and its records is in PRO Records Information Leaflet 67, *Records of the Board of Ordnance.*

16.9   Ordnance Survey

Between 1790 and 1805 mapmaking was carried out by civilians working under the direction of Royal Engineer officers. In 1805 the civilians were formed into the Corps of Military Surveyors and Draughtsmen. The Corps was disbanded in 1817 and the previous system reinstated. A card index containing the names of men who served either in the Corps or as civilians is held by the PRO Map Department at Kew. The index is based on information in WO 54/208 and other documents, and contains details of appointments and promotions.

From 1824 a number of survey companies, initially from the Royal Corps of Sappers and Miners and later from the Royal Engineers, were set up to help with the work of the Survey. The records of these men can be found in exactly the same way as those of other servicemen. For further details see sections 6 and 9 above.

A list of Royal Engineer officers who served in the Survey between 1791 and 1927 is in OS 1/1. A register of soldiers who died while serving with 13 Survey Company between 1829 and 1859 is in OS 3/300. This gives information about the cause of death and disposal of personal effects. OS 1/1/4 contains a list of all Royal Engineers serving with the Survey on 1 July 1890. A register of marriages of men in 16 Survey Company between 1901 and 1929, together with the birth dates of any children, is in OS 3/ 41. OS 3/275-277 contains seniority lists between 1935 and 1942. Further information may be found in PRO Records Information Leaflet 93, *Records of the Ordnance Survey.*

6.10 Prisoners of war (POWs)

Pre-1914

There are few records for men in the British Army who were prisoners before 1914. WO 40/2 contains a list of British and American POWs drawn up in 1781 with a view to exchange. Other lists are in T 64. Lists and accounts of British POWs in France and elsewhere for the period between 1793 and 1814, transmitted by the agent for prisoners in Paris, are among the registers of POWs in ADM 103. They appear, however, to cover largely naval and civilian internees. A list of POWs at Valenciennes between 805 and 1813 is in WO 25/2409. British POWs taken in the Crimea and by the Boers between 1899 and 1902 are listed in the *London Gazette*, but these lists are incomplete and generally name only officers, arranged under regiments.

First World War

AIR 1/892 contains lists of British and dominion POWs held in Germany, Turkey and Switzerland in 1916. A list of British and Dominion army POWs in German camps, specially the one at Giessen, in July 1915 is in ADM 1/8420/124. Interviews and reports of the Committee on the Treatment of British Prisoners of War between 1915 and 1919 are in WO 161/95-101. They are closed for 75 years. There is a substantial amount about POWs in the General Correspondence of the Foreign Office (FO 371) and a specific class of records dealing with POWs (FO 383), although few files relating to individuals survive. Deaths while a prisoner are recorded in registers held at St Catherine's House.

A list of officer POWs was compiled by the military agents Cox and Co in 1919 called *List of Officers taken prisoner in the various Theatres of War between August 1914 and November 1918.* It was reprinted in 1988 and is available in the Reference Room at Kew.

Second World War

Again, there are no central lists of British soldiers who were POWs. Information about individuals may occasionally be found among War Office files in WO 32 (code 91), and WO 219/1402, 1448-1474. The War Diary of MI 9, the division of Military Intelligence which dealt with escaped prisoners of all services, is in WO 165/ 39, and its papers are in WO 208/3242-3566. Medical reports on conditions in POW camps, with some reports on escapes, are among the Medical Historians Papers in WC 222/1352-1393. Further reports and lists of men sometimes occur in the Judge Advocate General's war crimes papers in WO 235, WO 309, WO 310, WO 311, WC 325, WO 331, WO 344, WO 356 and WO 367.

The International Committee of the Red Cross in Geneva keeps lists of all known POW: and internees of all nationalities for the Second World War. Enquiries within the Unite Kingdom concerning these lists should be sent to: The Director, International Welfar Department, British Red Cross Society, 9 Grosvenor Crescent, London SW1X 7EJ.

Korea

Lists of British and Commonwealth POWs of all services, between January 1951 and July 1953, are in WO 208/3999. The Historical Records and Reports on the Korean War in WO 308/54 also contain a list of Commonwealth prisoners compiled in January 1954.

Further information may be found in PRO Records Information Leaflets 72, *Prisoners of War: documents to 1919 in the Public Record Office* and 111, *Prisoners of War and Displaced Persons, 1939-1953.*

16.11   Royal Marines

Marines were raised in 1664 as land soldiers to serve on ships. Royal Marines were never under the control of the Army, but were always the responsibility of the Roya Navy. As a result there are very few records relating to the Marines in War Office classes. Marine records of interest to genealogists in Admiralty (ADM) classes are covered in PRO Information Leaflet 74, *Royal Marine records in the Public Record Office.*

16.12   Schools and Colleges

The Duke of York's Royal Military School was founded in 1802 as The Royal Military Asylum for Children of Soldiers of the Regular Army. It assumed its present name in 1892. Admission and discharge books for children from 1803 to 1923 are in WO 143. 17-25, with an index of admissions, 1910-1958, in WO 143/26. An apprenticeship book for the period 1806 to 1848 is in WO 143/52. Summaries of offences committed by boys, 1852-1879, are in WO 143/53-58. A record of admissions to the School, 1906-1956, is in WO 143/70.

A similar school, the Royal Hibernian Military School, was set up in Ireland in 1769 It was amalgamated with the Duke of York's School in 1924. Many of its records were destroyed by enemy action in 1940. An index of admissions to the School drawn up in 1863, with retrospective entries to about 1803 and annotations to approximately 1919 is in WO 143/27.

Records of the Royal Military Academy, Woolwich and the Royal Military College, Sandhurst, which provide professional training for officers, are available to the public at Sandhurst.

17.   FIRST WORLD WAR

17.1   Background reading

A very helpful introduction to tracing ancestors who fought during the First World War is Norman Holding, *World War I army ancestry* (FFHS, 1991). He has also written *More sources of World War I army ancestry* (FFHS, 1991) and *The location of British Army records: a national directory of World War I sources* (FFHS, 1991). Victor Neuburg, *A guide to the Western Front: A companion for Travellers* (London, 1988) is both a valuable introduction to the organization of the Army and a guide to the battlefields of Flanders and France during the First World War. An interesting account of life in the trenches is in Dennis Winter, *Death's men* (London, 1978).

17.2   Service records

No service records for either officers or other ranks have yet been transferred to the Public Record Office.

Officers

Registers and indexes of officers' services will be put into classes WO 338-WO 340 shortly. It is expected that these documents will be closed for 75 years from the last date of entry in each volume. Officers are, of course, listed in the Army Lists and in the list of officer POWs described in section 16.10 above.

Other ranks

It is difficult to know exactly how many service records of other ranks were destroyed or irreparably damaged by enemy action in 1942. Current estimates, however, suggest that about forty per cent of these records survive. Copying of those ready for transfer into WO 363 and WO 364 has begun, but it is expected that this work will take some years to complete.

Records of both officers and other ranks are held by the Ministry of Defence, CS(R)2b, Bourne Avenue, Hayes, Middlesex, UB3 1RF. The Ministry can release information from service records only with the written permission of the next of kin. A non-refundable fee, currently £15, is charged for all enquiries.

17.3 Casualty records

A list of men, arranged by regiment, who died during the war was published in *Soldiers who died in the Great War* (80 vols, HMSO 1921). There is a similar volume for officers who died during the war. Microfilmed copies of these publications are kept in the Microfilm Reading Room at Kew.

A roll of honour for men of the London Stock Exchange who served in the forces is kept in the Reference Room at Kew. Lists of employees of the Midland Railway who were either wounded or killed in action are in RAIL 491/1259. A similar roll of honour for men of the London, Brighton and South Coast Railway is in RAIL 414/761 and for the North Eastern Railway in RAIL 527/993. For an example of this see figure 16 on page 80.

French and Belgian death certificates for British soldiers who died in hospitals or elsewhere outside the immediate war zone between 1914 and 1920 are in RG 35/45-69. They are arranged by first letter of surname and are <u>at Chancery Lane</u>.

The Commonwealth War Graves Commission records all soldiers who died, or who were reported missing in action, during the war. Their records indicate the unit with which the soldier was serving and his place of burial. Their address is: Commonwealth War Graves Commission, 2 Marlow Road, Maidenhead SL6 7DX.

17.4 Medical and disability records

A selection of case files, covering a cross-section of disability pensions awarded after the First World War, is in PIN 26, but they are closed to public inspection for 50 years. MH 106 contains a specimen collection of admission and discharge registers from hospitals, casualty clearing stations and the like. The class also contains some medical cards for individuals, including the Queen Mary's Auxiliary Ambulance Corps (see section 17.9 below).

Ledgers of the payment of disability retired pay during and after the First World War are in PMG 42. Ledgers for supplementary allowances and special grants to officers, their widows and dependents are in PMG 43. Those for pensions to relatives of deceased officers are in PMG 44, widows' pensions in PMG 45, children's allowances in PMG 46, and pay to relatives of missing officers in PMG 47.

17.5 Medal rolls

Copies of rolls of awards of the British War Medal, Victory Medal, 1914 Star, 1914-1915 Star, Territorial Force War Medal, and Silver War Badge are in WO 329. They are awards to officers and other ranks of the Army, including nurses, and to the Royal Flying Corps. There is a card index on microfiche, in the Microfilm Reading Room at Kew, to all men who received these medals, arranged by name. The rolls themselves give the unit the man served in, his service number, the theatres of war he served in, and the medals to which he was entitled. In most cases the card index contains as much information as the medal roll.

The medal roll for the Military Medal has yet to be transferred to the PRO. When it has been it will be in WO 326.

Card indexes are also available in the Microfilm Reading Room at Kew to recipients of the following gallantry medals: Distinguished Conduct Medal, Meritorious Service Medal, and Military Medal, and to individuals mentioned in despatches. The cards give a reference to the *London Gazette* in which the award was gazetted. Sometimes a full citation was printed in the *Gazette* for the Distinguished Conduct Medal. Very occasionally a citation is given in full for the award of the Military Medal. Copies of the *London Gazette* are in ZJ 1.

Supplements to the Monthly Army Lists contain lists of recipients of medals. No date of or reason for the award is given, however. Lists of foreign awards to individuals are also included. Some records of these awards are in FO 371. Complete lists of all recipients of medals are given in the Supplements to the Monthly Army Lists during 1919.

7.6 War Diaries

From 1907 units on active service were required by the Field Service Regulations to keep a daily record of events. These records were called War Diaries or, occasionally, the Intelligence Summaries. The diaries contain daily reports on operations, intelligence reports and other pertinent material. A substantial number of maps, once included in these diaries, have been extracted and are now in WO 153. Many diaries are difficult to read because they were often scribbled in pencil in haste, using abbreviations which are now difficult to decipher, or they may be the third copy of a triplicate. For an example see figure 15 on page 79.

Most of these diaries are in WO 95. Certain war diaries containing particularly confidential material are in WO 154. They are closed for 75 years. Access is permitted provided that an undertaking not to reveal details of a personal nature is signed. These undertaking forms are available at the Reference Room desk at Kew.

The diaries are those of British and colonial units serving in theatres of operations between 1914 and 1922, principally France and Flanders, but also Italy, Mesopotamia, Palestine, Salonika, Russia, home and colonial forces, and of the post-war armies of occupation. They are arranged by theatre of operations and then by army, corps and division.

Provided that the unit is known, these war diaries can be a useful way of fleshing out the career of a man during the war. It is unusual, however, for a war diary to mention individuals, unless they are officers. Periods of combat are also likely to be described only in brief, and deaths of men or examples of gallantry may not be mentioned. Where a unit served can be traced through the Orders of Battle in WO 95/5467-5494.

7.7 Royal Flying Corps

Until the creation of the Royal Air Force on 1 April 1918 the Royal Flying Corps (RFC) was part of the Army. Many men were recruited into the RFC from other parts of the Army. A selection of RFC squadron, and other unit, records is in AIR 1. They can contain a great deal of valuable information about individuals, especially officers and aircrew, but only a relatively small number survive.

There is a muster roll of other ranks serving in the RFC on 1 April 1918 in AIR 1/819. Another copy is in AIR 10/232-237. There are several series of casualty reports from the Western Front for the period April 1916 to November 1918 in AIR 1/843-860, 914-916 and 960-969. Medals awarded to RFC personnel are in WO 329. For further details see section 17.5 above. Officers are also listed in the Army Lists.

Casualty record cards for men of the RFC, killed or wounded during the war, are held by the RAF Museum, Hendon, London NW9 5LL.

Further information is given in PRO Records Information Leaflet 13, *Air Records as Sources for Biography and Family History*.

17.8   Conscientious objectors

After the introduction of conscription in 1915-1916 men could appeal against army service through the Military Service Tribunals. Most records of these tribunals were destroyed after the war. Records for the Middlesex Service Tribunal were preserved, however, and now are in MH 47, and records of a few other Tribunals are held at local record offices.

17.9   Women in the war

As the war progressed women came to do a number of the jobs previously done by men, such as driving, although they did not take part in actual combat. Correspondence about the employment of women in the Army is to be found in WO 32 (code 68) and WO 162/30-73. These papers contain very little of a genealogical nature.

The Women's Army Auxiliary Corps was formed in 1917 and became the Queen Mary's Army Auxiliary Corps in May 1918. An incomplete nominal roll for the Corps is in WO 162/16. A list of women motor drivers employed in the Women's Army Auxiliary Corps during the war is in WO 162/62. Recommendations for honours are in WO 162/65. War diaries for the Corps in France between 1917 and 1919 are in WO 95/84-85. Many women served as nurses or otherwise helped in hospitals or elsewhere in the medical services. Records of nurses are described in section 16.7 above. Lists of nurses arriving in France during the war are given in WO 95/3982.

Some medical sheets for members of the Voluntary Aid Detachment and Queen Mary's Auxiliary Ambulance Corps during the First World War are in MH 106/2207-2211. Registers of disability and retired pay between 1917 and 1919 are in PMG 42/1-12.

Further information is contained in PRO Records Information Leaflet 120, *Military nurses and nursing services: record sources in the Public Record Office*.

18.   SECOND WORLD WAR
18.1   Service records

As with the First World War, Army service records are not yet at the Public Record Office. They are unlikely to be transferred for many years. For details about how to gain access to them see section 17.2 above. A roll of honour for men and women who died during the war is in WO 304.

18.2   Casualty returns

Retrospective registers of deaths from enemy action in the Far East between 1941 and 1945 are in RG 33/11, 132, with an index in RG 43/14. <u>These records are at Chancery Lane.</u>
Indexed death registers for the war are at St Catherine's House.
The Commonwealth War Graves Commission records all soldiers who died, or who were reported missing in action, during the Second World War, as for the First. For details see section 17.3 above.

18.3   War diaries

These usually give a much fuller description of the units' activities than their counterparts of the First World War. They often include a detailed narrative of the operations of the unit, together with daily orders, maps and other miscellaneous material. It is unusual for the diaries to contain details about the deaths of, or acts of bravery by, individual men especially those serving in the other ranks. Nominal rolls, or lists, of officers are sometimes included.
Most war diaries are closed for 100 years, but special permission can be obtained to see them by signing an undertaking agreeing not to disclose items relating to individuals. Undertaking forms are obtained from the Reference Room desk at Kew. The war diaries are arranged as follows:

Theatre of operation/force	Class
British Expeditionary Force (France, 1939-1940)	WO 167
Central Mediterranean Forces (Italy and Greece, 1943-1946)	WO 170
Dominion Forces	WO 179
GHQ Liaison Regiment	WO 215
Home Forces	WO 166
Madagascar	WO 174
Medical services (ie hospitals, field ambulances etc)	WO 177
Middle East Forces (Egypt, Libya, invasion of Sicily and Italy)	WO 169
Military missions	WO 178
North Africa	WO 175

(Tunisia and Algeria, 1941-1943)

North West Expeditionary Force	WO 168
(Norway, 1940)	
North West Europe	WO 171
(France, Belgium, Holland and Germany, 1944-1946)	
South East Asia	WO 172
(India, Burma,Malaya)	
Special Services	WO 218
Various smaller theatres	WO 176
War Office Directorates	WO 165
West Africa	WO 173

Orders of Battle in WO 212 show where units served.

18.4   Home Guard

The PRO holds few papers about the Home Guard, or Local Defence Volunteers as it was first known. A list of Home Guard officers compiled in 1944 is in WO 199/3212-3217. WO 199 also contains other records about the Home Guard.

Most surviving records, however, are held by local record offices.

Attestation papers for the Home Guard are held by the Army Medal Office, Government Buildings, Worcester Road, Droitwich, Worcs WR9 8AU. The Office will release information only to next of kin, but can help only if the battalion of the person sought is given.

A *Home Guard List* similar to the Army List is held by the Imperial War Museum. L B Whittaker has recently compiled *Stand down: Orders of battle for the units of the Home Guard of the United Kingdom, November 1944* (Newport, Gwent, 1990) which may be of use in tracing units.

18.5   Medals

No medal rolls for the Second World War have yet been transferred to the Public Record Office. They are held by the Army Medal Office, Droitwich (for full address see section 18.4 above). Citations for the Victoria Cross are in CAB 106/312. Citations for awards of gallantry and distinguished service medals are in WO 373. Citations were sometimes published in the *London Gazette,* copies of which are in ZJ 1.

18.6   Women in the war

As in the First World War women played a major role in the Army, undertaking many duties which would normally be done by men. Correspondence about the employment of women in the Army is to be found in WO 32 (code 68) and WO 162/30-73. These papers contain very little of a genealogical nature.

Some women served in the Auxiliary Territorial Service (ATS). A few war diaries for the ATS are to be found in WO 166.

Many women served as nurses during the war. War diaries for hospitals and medical units are in WO 177. Each unit also submitted reports, usually of a technical nature, to the War Office. These are in WO 222.

19. OTHER TWENTIETH CENTURY CAMPAIGNS AND THE PEACETIME ARMY

19.1 War diaries

Apart from the two world wars, the British Army has taken part in a number of operations during this century. The main source of interest for family historians will be the war diaries of participating units. References are:

Campaign	Class
Abyssinia (1935-1936)	WO 191
Egypt (1935-1936)	WO 191
India (1930-1937)	WO 191
Korea (1950-1953)	WO 281
Palestine (1936-1938, 1945-1948)	WO 191
Shanghai (1927-1932)	WO 191
Suez (1956)	WO 288

19.2 Quarterly Historical Reports

Between 1946 and 1950, army units compiled Quarterly Historical Reports. They are similar in format to war diaries, but are not as detailed. The references are:

Area	Class
British Army of the Rhine	WO 267
British Element Trieste Force	WO 264
British Troops Austria	WO 263
Caribbean	WO 270
Central Mediterranean Forces	WO 262
East and West Africa	WO 269
Far East	WO 268
Gibraltar	WO 266
Home Forces	WO 271
Malta	WO 265
Middle East (including Palestine)	WO 261

Quarterly Historical Reports were replaced by the Unit Historical Record in 1950; these are in WO 305. Operation Record Books for the Army Air Corps from 1957 are in WO 295. A list of men killed or wounded during the Easter Rising in Dublin in 1916 is in WO 35/69.

APPENDIX 1

ORGANIZATIONAL CHART OF THE ARMY

This chart gives a very brief guide to the organization of the Army as it was between 1881 and 1945.

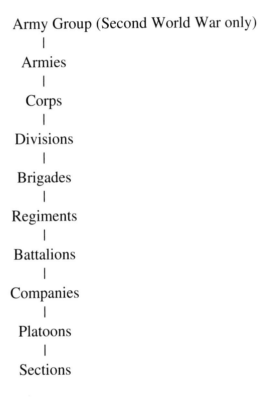

Army Group (Second World War only)
|
Armies
|
Corps
|
Divisions
|
Brigades
|
Regiments
|
Battalions
|
Companies
|
Platoons
|
Sections

APPENDIX 2

RANKS OF THE BRITISH ARMY

Commissioned Officers
Field Marshal
General
Lieutenant General
Major General
Brigadier
Colonel
Lieutenant Colonel
Major
Captain
Lieutenant
2nd Lieutenant

Non-commissioned officers and other ranks
Warrant Officer 1st Class
Warrant Officer 2nd Class
Sergeant Major
Staff Sergeant
Sergeant
Corporal
Lance Corporal
Private

This is a very simplified table. Various branches and regiments have tended to give different names to different ranks. For example, in the Royal Artillery a Private is called a Gunner, in the Royal Engineers he is a Sapper, and in Cavalry regiments he may be called a Trooper.

APPENDIX 3

USEFUL DATES

Campaigns and wars

1642-1649	English Civil War
1660 May 25	Restoration of Charles I
1688	Glorious revolution
1701-1713	War of Spanish Succession
1704 Aug 13	Battle of Blenheim
1715	Jacobite rebellion
1740-1748	War of Austrian Succession
1745	Jacobite rebellion
1756 May 3- 1763 Feb 10	Seven Years War
1775-1783	American War of Independence
1789	French revolution
1793 Feb 1- 1815 Jun 22	Napoleonic Wars (or French Revolutionary Wars)
1808 Aug 1- 1814 Mar 30	Peninsular Campaign
1815 Jun 18	Battle of Waterloo
1812 Jun 19- 1815 Jan 8	Second Anglo-American War (War of 1812)
1854 Sept 14- 1856 Mar 30	Crimean War
1854 Oct 25	Charge of the Light Brigade
1857 May 10-Dec 6	Indian Mutiny
1860, 1862-1864	Maori Wars in New Zealand
1878-1879	Zulu War
1879 Jan 22	Massacre of British Troops at Isandhlwana, Zululand
1878-1881	First South African (Boer) War
1881 Feb 27	Defeat of British troops at Majuba Hill, South Africa
1882-1885	Egyptian and Sudan Campaigns
1885 Jan 29	Capture of Khartoum
1898	Sudan campaign
1899 Oct 12- 1902 May 31	Second South African (Boer) War
1900 Feb 28	Relief of Ladysmith, South Africa
1900 May 17	Relief of Mafeking, South Africa

1914 Aug 4- 1918 Nov 11	First World War
1914 Aug 22-23	Battle of Mons
1915 Apr 25- 1916 Jan 8	Gallipoli campaign, Turkey
1916 July 1- Nov 8	Battle of the Somme
1917 Jul 31- Nov 10	Battle of Passchendaele (Third Battle of Ypres)
1916 Apr 24- May 1	Easter Rising, Dublin
1922 Dec 17	Last British troops leave Southern Ireland
1939 Sept 3 - 1945 Sept 2	Second World War
1940 May 27- June 4	Evacuation from Dunkirk
1941 Apr 22 - May 29	Greek and Crete campaigns
1942 Feb 15	Surrender of Singapore
1942 Oct 23	Start of Battle of El Alamein
1943 Jul 10	Allies land in Sicily
1944 Jun 6	Allies land in France (D-Day)
1945 May 8	Germans surrender (VE-Day)
1945 Aug 14	Surrender of Japan (VJ-Day)
1947 Aug 15	Last British troops leave India
1948 May 14	Last British troops leave Palestine
1950 Jun 26- 1953 Jul 27	Korean War
1956 Oct 31- Nov 7	Suez Crisis

Army history

1645 Jan 6	Formation of New Model Army
1661	Britain's oldest regiment, the Coldstream Guards, formed
1664	Royal Marines established
1684	Admission of first pensioners to the Royal Hospital Kilmainham, Ireland
1692	Admission of first pensioners to the Royal Hospital Chelsea
1708	Provision of pensions to widows of officers
1716	Royal Artillery founded
1717	Corps of Engineers founded
1740	First publication of the Army List
1757	Militia Act revives local militias
1760	Institution of soldiers' pension documents
1787	Corps of Engineers becomes Royal Engineers
1796	Establishment of Army Chaplains Department
1810	Army Medical Department established
1811	Royal Corps of Miners and Sappers set up

1833	Long Service and Good Conduct Medal instituted
1839-1915	Hart's Army Lists
1854	Institution of Distinguished Conduct Medal
1855 May 25	Ordnance Board abolished
1856 Jan 29	Victoria Cross instituted
1857	Army Hospital Corps formed
1859	Volunteer regiments formed
1867	Second Class Army Reserve established
1870	Army Enlistment Act introduces of short service engagements of 12 years for other ranks
1870	Abolition of purchase of commission
1881	Abolition of numbered regiments of foot and their re-establishment as regiments with county affiliations
1881	Army Nursing Service formed
1886	Institution of Distinguished Service Order
1898	Royal Army Medical Corps formed by merger of Army Medical Department and Army Medical Staff Corps
1913	Last date for soldiers' documents in the PRO
1918 April 1	Formation of Royal Air Force from Royal Flying Corps and Royal Naval Air Service
1922 Dec 6	Irish regiments disbanded on independence of Irish Free State
1940-1944	Home Guard (Local Defence Volunteers)

APPENDIX 4

RECORDS HELD BY OTHER INSTITUTIONS

Local record offices

Relatively few military records are held by local record offices. Those that are, however, are often of great interest to the family historian. Three different types of military records may be held by a local record office.

Firstly, there are records created by local units, either volunteers or the regular army. These may consist of service rolls, war diaries and internal records of the unit and can give an insight into the life of the service. Records of some territorial and auxiliary forces associations have been deposited at local record offices and may contain items of interest to family historians. Details of these records, for the First World War period, are in Norman Holding, *The location of British Army records: a national directory of World War I sources* (FFHS, 1991).

Local record offices also hold records of local militia units. In particular, militia lists (of all men) and militia enrolment lists (of men chosen to serve) may survive for the period 1758 to 1831. These records, and others likely to be of use to the family historian, are described in Jeremy Gibson and Mervyn Medlycott, *Militia lists and musters, 1757-1876* (FFHS, 1990).

Records relating to military events, although not military records as such, include rolls of honour for men who served during the world wars, or lists of casualties taken from local newspapers. Photographs of parades and manoeuvres may also be held locally.

Brief details of the holdings of most record repositories in Britain are given in Janet Foster and Julia Sheppard, *British archives: a guide to archive resources in the United Kingdom* (2nd edition, 1988). The addresses of local record offices, together with times of opening, are given in *Record repositories in Great Britain* (9th edition, HMSO, 1991). Similar information is included in Jeremy Gibson, *Record offices: how to find them* (FFHS, 1991), together with maps and other details.

Imperial War Museum

The Imperial War Museum has a very large collection of private diaries, letters, papers and unpublished memoirs for all ranks in the Army from 1914 to the present. The Museum also maintains a comprehensive series of biographical files on persons decorated with the Victoria Cross or the George Cross since the inception of the awards. The address is:

Imperial War Museum
Lambeth Road
London
SE1 6HZ
(071-735 8922)

British Library, Oriental and India Office Collections (formerly India Office Library and Records (IOLR))

The IOLR hold very large collections of material relating to the British in India. They also hold 1,000 volumes of births, marriages and deaths returns between c.1683 and 1947. There are indexes to these records.

Further information about their holdings of use to the genealogist may be found in Ian A. Baxter, *A brief guide to biographical sources*, produced by the IOLR in 1979. The address is:

British Library, Oriental and India Office Collections
197 Blackfriars Road
London
SE1 8NG
(071-412 7873)

National Army Museum

The Museum has a large collection of private, regimental and related papers concerning the British Army, the Indian Army prior to 1947, and British colonial forces to relevant dates of independence.

The life of the ordinary soldier is well illustrated by letters, diaries, memoirs and poems written by men stationed in every corner of the globe. There is a fine representative collection of commissions of officers for both the British and Indian armies.

The Museum holds regimental records for the 9th/12th Royal Lancers, Westminster Dragoons, Surrey Yeomanry, and various Indian Army units, together with documents relating to the Irish regiments of the British Army disbanded upon the formation of the Irish Free State in 1922: the Royal Irish Regiment, Connaught Rangers, Leinster Regiment, Royal Munster Fusiliers, and the Royal Dublin Fusiliers. Of particular interest to the family historian is the card index of biographical information on officers of the East India Company compiled by Major Vernon Hodson.

In addition, it holds a comprehensive record of all military casualties from 1900 to the present day, giving next of kin, address and how personal possessions and money were dispersed.

The Museum also has a very large library of regimental histories, military biographies and Army Lists, together with collections of photographs and sound recordings of old soldiers. The address is:

National Army Museum
Royal Hospital Road
London
SW3 4HT
(071-730 0717)

Regimental museums

Many regiments have a museum, some of which have collections of records which could be of use to the family historian.

Terence Wise, *A guide to military museums* (Doncaster, 1986) gives the addresses of museums. In addition, Norman Holding, *The location of British Army records* (FFHS, 1991) lists museums and gives some idea of the records that each one holds relating to the First World War.

Office of Population Censuses and Surveys (General Register Office)

The OPCS holds Chaplains' returns between 1796 and 1880 recording births, baptisms, marriages, and deaths of army personnel and their families. They are generally for army stations abroad. There is a similar series of registers, 1761-1924, for births, baptisms, marriages, deaths and burials of soldiers and their families at home and abroad. There is an index to births and baptisms.

The Registrar General also holds the Army Register Books, 1881-1959, containing births, marriages and deaths outside the UK. Births, marriages and deaths from 1959 for the Army, Royal Navy and Royal Air Force are combined together in a single register. There is a unified index from 1964.

St Catherine's House also has indexes to deaths in both world wars, and for the South African War (1899-1902).

Fees, similar to those charged for copies of ordinary certificates, are payable. The address is:

General Register Office
St Catherine's House
10 Kingsway
London
WC2B 6JP

Postal applications for certificates should be sent to:

Office of Population Censuses and Surveys
General Register Office
Postal Application Section
Smedley Hydro
Trafalgar Road
Birkdale
Southport
Merseyside
PR8 2HH

Scotland

Certain registers relating to deaths of warrant officers, NCOs and men in the South African War (1899-1902) are held at the General Register Office for Scotland, New Register House, Edinburgh EH1 3YT. They also hold an incomplete set of birth, marriage and death registers for Scottish armed forces for the Second World War.

Ireland

Birth, marriage and death registers created under the Army Act 1879 for the period between 1880 and 1921 are held by the General Register Office, Joyce House, 8-11 Lombard Street, Dublin 2.

Society of Genealogists

The library of the Society has a number of useful books, including regimental histories and rolls of honour. In addition, the Society has produced leaflets on *Army muster and description books*, *Army research: selected biography* and *In search of a soldier ancestor*. The address is:

Society of Genealogists
14 Charterhouse Buildings
Goswell Road
London
EC1M 7BA
(071-251 8799)

APPENDIX 5

FURTHER READING

The best general introduction to family history in the Public Record Office is Amanda Bevan and Andrea Duncan, *Tracing Your ancestors in the Public Record Office* (4th edition, HMSO, 1990). Section 18 in the book covers many of the classes of military records of genealogical interest in the PRO.

The Office also produces a number of Records Information Leaflets on many subjects of interest to the family historian. The leaflets are intended to be used at the PRO in conjunction with the records. They are available free of charge to those visiting the Office. The PRO is unable to supply leaflets by post. Those relating to military records are:

Title	Leaflet Number
Operational records of the British Army in the First World War	6
Operational records of the British Army in the Second World War	7
Militia muster rolls, 1522-1640	46
British Army records as sources for biography and genealogy	59
Operational records of the British Army, 1660-1914	61
Records of the Board of Ordnance	67
Prisoners of War: documents to 1919 in the Public Record Office	72
Royal Marine records in the Public Record Office	74
Records of courts martial: Army	84
Records of the Ordnance Survey	93
Service medal and award rolls: First World War	101
Indexes to medal entitlement: First World War	105
Records of medals	108
Prisoners of war and displaced persons, 1939-1953	111
Military nurses and nursing services: record sources in the Public Record Office	120
Armed service pension records: Army	123
The Militia since 1757	126

In addition, there are a number of source sheets which aim to provide searchers with lists of references on popular topics. They include:

Title	Number
Ireland, 1920-1922	6
The Zulu War	10
Home Guard	14
D-Day (Operation Overlord)	20

Stella Colwell, *Family Roots* (London, 1991) gives many examples of military records to be found at the PRO and includes a brief account of finding ancestors who served in the Army. An idiosyncratic account of how to trace individuals in Army records is Gerald Hamilton-Edwards, *In search of army ancestry* (Chichester, 1977). The Society of Genealogists will shortly be publishing Michael J Watts, *My Ancestor was in the British Army - How can I find out more about him?* R H Montague, *How to trace your military ancestors in Australia and New Zealand* (Sydney, 1989) is a useful illustrated guide to military records of value to genealogists in Australia and New Zealand. Many queries about military records are answered in F C Markwell and Pauline Saul, *The family historian's enquire within* (3rd edition, FFHS, 1991).

There are several general histories of the British Army which can provide background information for the family historian, such as David Ascoli, *A companion to the British Army, 1660-1983* (London, 1983). A useful introduction to the organization of the Army before 1914 is given in John M. Kitzmiller II, *In search of the 'forlorn hope': a comprehensive guide to locating British regiments and their records, 1640 to World War One* (2 vols, Salt Lake City, 1988). A good general history of the British Army is Corelli Barnett, *Britain and her army* (London, 1970).

An interesting account of the life of the soldier is Victor Neuburg, *Gone for a soldier* (London, 1989). Byron Farwell, *For Queen and country: a social history of the Victorian and Edwardian army* (London, 1981) is a well written introduction to the life many ancestors must have experienced. A pictorial introduction to the life of the Scottish soldier is Jenni Calder, *The story of the Scottish soldier, 1600-1914* (HMSO, 1987). PRO publications, and those of the Federation of Family History Societies (FFHS), are on sale at the PRO shops at Kew and Chancery Lane.

Reference		WO 97

WO 97	**Date** 1760-1854	**Description**
		13th Foot
341		Abb - Car
342		Carr - Dav
343		Davi - Gre
344		Gree - Kyl
345		Lac - Mur
346		Nag - Ric
347		Rich - Spe
348		Ste - You
		14th Foot
349		Abb - Bra
350		Brad - Cla
351		Cle - Dru
352		Eas - Gra
353		Gre - Hyn
354		Ill - Kno
355		Lad - Mat
356		Matt - Pee
357		Peet - Sau
358		Sax - Swa
359		Swi - Wal
360		Walt - You
		15th Foot
361		Abs - Car
362		Carr - Eva
363		Eve - Hug
364		Hul - Lyo
365		McA - Owe
366		Pac - Ste
367		Stew - You
		16th Foot
368		Abb - Cas
369		Cash - Cus
370		Dak - Fle
371		Flo - Hea
372		Hef - Law
373		Laws - Mal
374		Man - Qui
375		Rab - Sul
376		Sut - Yox

Figure 1. A class list

229 | 230 | 231

Line Battalions.

5 F.—*continued.*

Frederic R. Carleton 13July67
Chas. Herbert Broad, *I. of M.* 12Oct.67
Charles Hackett 16Oct.67
2W. FitzAllan Way 22Aug.68
2Josiah W. Pearse-Hobbs, *I. of M.* 3Feb.69
1Geo. Wm. Hargreave, *d.* 27Feb.69
2H. Aitken Cherry, *adj.* 27Feb.69
2Fred. Wm. Saunders 5Jan.70
1Geo. Hart Dyke 19Jan.70
1Edw. Le M. Trafford 9Apr.70
1Henry Kilgour 8June70
2Chas. Geo. Heathcote 30Nov.70
2Reginald H. Thurlow 24Dec.70
1James Sinclair Cramsie 22Feb.71
2Robt. Milnes Thornton 22Mar.71
1Herbert Reay Gall 28Oct.71
2Middleton W. Biddulph 28Oct.71
2Richard Williamson 28Oct.71
1Samuel Boxwell 28Oct.71
2Robt. Auld 28Oct.71
1Thos. Arthur Campion 28Oct.71
1Alexr. Chancellor, *d.* 28Oct.71
2Percy Fra. Lambart 28Oct.71
2Harris England Buchanan 28Oct.71
2Hen. Hanbury Davies 28Oct.71
2Chas. L. S. Auber 28Oct.71
1Geo. Nevile Wyatt 28Oct.71
1Chas. G. C. Money 29May72
2Hen. Mordaunt Matthew 3July74

Sub Lieutenants.

1Hen. Beaufoy Thornhill 23Apr.73
1Geo. Atkins Collins 13June74

Paymasters.

1Fred. Blanco Forster, *m.* 5Dec.51
lt. 13Oct.48
2Joshua J. Bowness 14Oct.68
21Aug.67

Instrs. of Musk.

2J. W. Pearse-Hobbs, *lt.* 13May72
1C. H. Broad, *lt.* 25Apr.73

Adjutants.

1W. S. Darley, *lt.* 5Aug.67
2H. A. Cherry, *lt.* 26June72

Quar. Masters.

1Fra. Drake 17Nov.57
2Michael Downey 4Oct.73

Medical Officers.

1A. M. Tippetts, *sur. m.* 15June66
2C. F. Pollock, *M.B., sur.*

Scarlet—Facings bright green.

Ag. Messrs. Cox & Co.
Ir. Ag. Sir E. Borough, *Bt.* & Co.

6th (Royal First Warwickshire).

1 Bn. .... *Bengal,*
Dep. .... *with* 2 *Bn.*
2 Bn. .... *Guernsey.*
Brigade, Sub-District and Brig. Dep.† (*Warwick*) } 28
(† *Not yet formed.*)

The Antelope.
The Rose and Crown.

"Roleia." "Vimiera."
"Corunna." "Vittoria."
"Pyrenees." "Nivelle."
"Orthes." "Peninsula."
"Niagara."

Colonel.

John ffolliott Crofton, *l.g.* 5Sept.69

Lt. Colonels.

Chas. O. Creagh-Osborne, C.B. *c., p.s.c., s.* 1Feb.67
2John H. F. Elkington, *c.* 27Nov.67
1Thos. Lynden Bell 1Apr.73

Majors.

2Henry B. Feilden 8June67
2Jas. N. Colthurst 30Aug.71
1Evan B. Gardyne 1Feb.73
1Wilsone Black, *p.s.c.* 1Apr.73

20 *Captains.*

2Lewis Blyth Hole, *m.* 29Sept.59
1Alfred Austin, *m., d.* 30Apr.61
2D. G. Protheroe 28Jan.62
1Wm. C. Wolseley 19Dec.62
1Dawson K. Evans 29May63
2Spencer Field 22Mar.64
2Jas. Geo. Cockburn 3May64
2Charles Whyte 9Mar.66
2H. Burrows Adcock 3July66
1Douglas Hastings, *l.c.* 15Mar.53
1Albert H. Harrison 8June67
1Chas. W. H. Wilson 14Sept.67
2Fredk. Helyar 14Oct.68
1Jas. FitzGerald 17Mar.69
2Jas. T. Nugent 19Jan.70
2Alex. C. Hall 28May70
1Jacob B. Hopkins 1Apr.73
2Hen. P. L'E. St. George 20Oct.69
1Wm. Grant, *s.* 24Sept.74
1Gust. W. B. Collis 27Feb.75

Lieutenants.

2Arthur Morton 19Dec.62
2Adol. R. A. Collis 1Dec.65

6 F.—*continued.*

2Geo. Sharp Grimble 9Mar.66
1David M. F. Brady 29May67
2Jas. Ruddle Gibbs, *I. of M.* 8June67
1Gerald de Courcy Morton 13July67
1Robert Stratford 2Aug.65
1Aug. Wm. Whitworth, *I. of M.* 14Sept.67
1Fred. Leigh Grundy 9Nov.67
2James Lewis, *adj.* 30Sept.68
1Richard Meredith 17Mar.69
2Hen. Deering Thomas 29May69
1Frank Lougbourne 28May70
2Neville Fredk. Mansergh 27Oct.71
2Gerald H. C. Stracey 28Oct.71
1Edward Arthur Ball 28Oct.71
1Arthur M. O'Beirne 28Oct.71
1Richd. John Doyne 28Oct.71
2Denman Croft Murray 28Oct.71
1Edwd. H. Corse-Scott 28Oct.71
1E. J. Winnington-Ingram 28Oct.71
2Willoughby E. G. Forbes 28Oct.71
1Hen. Blake Harward 28Oct.71
Chas. Boileau Down (*prob.*) 28Oct.71
1St. Geo. John Rathborne 28Oct.71
1Thos. Geo. Lumsden 15Jan.73
2Thos. R. F. B. Hallowes 12Nov.73
2John Wm. Stevenson 2Dec.74

Sub Lieutenants.

1Valens C. Tonnochy 9Aug.73
2Wm. Erskine Scott 9Aug.73
2Gregory Haines 9Aug.73
2Gilbert M. Yaldwyn 9Aug.73
2Morey Quayle Jones 12Nov.73
1Hen. Lushington Ramsay 28Feb.74
1Wm. Conrad Faithfull 21Sept.74
1Chas. Edwd. Pollock 11Feb.75

Paymasters.

2†John O'Connor, *m.* 3Nov.57
qua. mast. 11Mar.53
1Wm. Wastell, *m.* 21Dec.60
lt. 26Jan.58

Instrs. of Musk.

2J. R. Gibbs, *lt.* 30Aug.70
1A. W. Whitworth, *lt.* 25Mar.71

Adjutants.

2J. Lewis, *lt.* 21Aug.72
1

Quarter Masters.

1Geo. Beedle 10July66
2Jas. B. Tippetts 4Oct.73

Medical Officers.

2F. J. Shortt, *sur. m.* 4Feb.71
1E. F. O'Leary, *M.D., sur. m.* 9Sept.71

Scarlet—Facings blue.

† *On duty in 66th Sub-Dist.*

Ag. Messrs. Cox & Co.
Ir. Ag. Sir E. Borough, *Bt.* & Co.

Figure 2 The Army List April 1875 Column 230 6th Foot

The Army List has been published continuously since 1754. It lists officers with the units to which they are attached. Other ranks and NCOs do not appear in it. The Army List can contain other information however such as the names of officers on half pay and where regiments are stationed.

The example here is a page from the Army List for April 1875. It lists all the Officers in the 6th Foot, with the dates of their being appointed to the rank. The first battalion was stationed in Bengal, the second on Guernsey. The Army List also describes the regimental badge and battle honours.

Note the entry for Captain William Wolseley. His service record may be found in figure 5. See also a similar entry from Hart's Army List in figure 3.

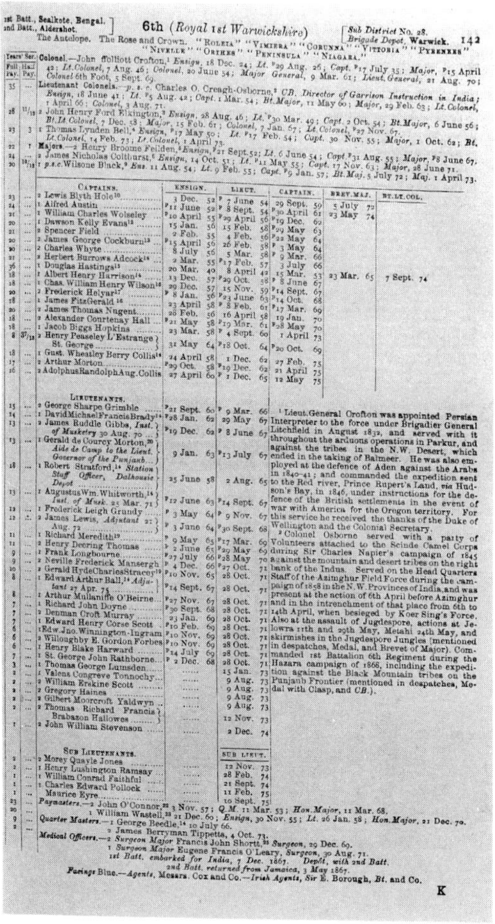

1st Batt., Sealkote, Bengal.
2nd Batt., Aldershot.

6th (*Royal 1st Warwickshire*)

Sub District No. 28.
Brigade Depot, **Warwick.** 142

The Antelope. The Rose and Crown. "Roleia" "Vimiera" "Corunna" "Vittoria" "Pyrenees" "Nivelle" "Orthes" "Peninsula" "Niagara."

Years' Ser. Full Pay	Half Pay	
		Colonel.—John ffolliott Crofton,[1] *Ensign*, 18 Dec. 24; *Lt.* P29 Aug. 26; *Capt.* P17 July 35; *Major*, P15 April 42; *Lt.Colonel*, 7 Aug. 46; *Colonel*, 20 June 54; *Major General*, 9 Mar. 61; *Lieut.General*, 21 Aug. 70; *Colonel* 6th Foot, 5 Sept. 69.
35	...	**Lieutenant Colonels.**—*p.s.c.* Charles O. Creagh-Osborne,[2] *CB. Director of Garrison Instruction in India*; *Ensign*, 18 June 41; *Lt.* P5 Aug. 42; *Capt.* 1 Mar. 54; *Bt.Major*, 11 May 60; *Major*, 29 Feb. 63; *Lt.Colonel*, 1 April 66; *Colonel*, 3 Aug. 71.
28	11/12	2 John Henry Ford Elkington,[3] *Ensign*, 28 Aug. 46; *Lt.* P30 Mar. 49; *Capt.* 2 Oct. 54; *Bt.Major*, 6 June 56; *Bt.Lt.Colonel*, 7 Dec. 58; *Major*, 15 Feb. 61; *Colonel*, 7 Jan. 67; *Lt.Colonel*, P27 Nov. 67.
23	3	1 Thomas Lynden Bell,[4] *Ensign*, P17 May 50; *Lt.* P17 Feb. 54; *Capt.* 30 Nov. 55; *Major*, 1 Oct. 62; *Bt.Lt.Colonel*, 14 Feb. 73; *Lt.Colonel*, 1 April 73.
22	1	**Majors.**—2 Henry Broome Feilden,[5] *Ensign*, P21 Sept. 52; *Lt.* 6 June 54; *Capt.* P31 Aug. 55; *Major*, P8 June 67.
24	...	2 James Nicholas Colthurst,[6] *Ensign*, 14 Oct. 51; *Lt.* P11 May 55; *Capt.* 17 Nov. 63; *Major*, 28 June 71.
20	10/12	1 *p.s.c.* Wilsone Black,[9] *Ens.* 11 Aug. 54; *Lt.* 9 Feb. 55; *Capt.* P9 Jan. 57; *Bt.Maj.* 5 July 72; *Maj.* 1 April 73.

Full Pay	Half Pay	Captains.	Ensign.	Lieut.	Captain.	Brev.Maj.	Bt.Lt.Col.
23	...	2 Lewis Blyth Hole[10]	3 Dec. 52	P 7 June 54	29 Sept. 59		
24	...	1 Alfred Austin	P11 June 52	P 8 Sept. 54	P30 April 61	5 July 72	
21	...	1 William Charles Wolseley	P10 April 55	P29 April 56	P19 Dec. 62	23 May 74	
20	...	1 Dawson Kelly Evans[12]	15 Jan. 56	15 Feb. 58	P29 May 63		
21	...	2 Spencer Field	2 Feb. 55	4 Feb. 56	P22 May 64		
20	...	2 James George Cockburn[13]	P15 April 56	26 Feb. 58	P 3 May 64		
20	...	2 Charles Whyte	8 July 56	5 Mar. 58	P 9 Mar. 66		
21	...	2 Herbert Burrows Adcock[14]	2 Mar. 55	P17 Feb. 57	3 July 66		
36	...	1 Douglas Hastings[15]	20 Mar. 40	8 April 42	15 Mar. 53	23 Mar. 65	7 Sept. 74
18	...	1 Albert Henry Harrison[14]	13 Dec. 57	P29 Oct. 58	P 8 June 67		
18	...	1 Chas. William Henry Wilson[16]	29 Dec. 57	15 Nov. 59	P14 Sept. 67		
20	...	2 Frederick Helyar[17]	P 8 Jan. 56	P23 June 63	P14 Oct. 68		
18	...	1 James FitzGerald[16]	23 April 58	P 8 Feb. 61	P17 Mar. 69		
20	...	2 James Thomas Nugent	28 Feb. 56	16 April 58	19 Jan. 70		
18	...	2 Alexander Courtenay Hall	P21 May 58	P19 Mar. 61	P28 May 70		
18	...	1 Jacob Biggs Hopkins	23 Mar. 58	P 4 Sept. 60	1 April 73		
8	37/12	2 Henry Peaseley L'Estrange St. George	31 May 64	P18 Oct. 64	P20 Oct. 69		
18	...	1 Gust. Wheatley Berry Collis[14]	24 April 58	1 Dec. 62	27 Feb. 75		
17	...	2 Arthur Morton	P29 Oct. 58	P19 Dec. 62	21 April 75		
16	...	2 Adolphus Randolph Aug. Collis	27 April 60	P 1 Dec. 65	12 May 75		

Full Pay	Half Pay	Lieutenants.	Ensign.	Lieut.
15	...	2 George Sharpe Grimble	P21 Sept. 60	P 9 Mar. 66
14	...	1 David Michael Francis Brady[14]	P28 Jan. 62	29 May 67
13	...	2 James Ruddle Gibbs, *Inst. of Musketry* 30 Aug. 70	P19 Dec. 62	P 8 June 67
13	...	1 Gerald de Courcy Morton,[20] *Aide de Camp to the Lieut. Governor of the Punjaub*	9 Jan. 63	P13 July 67
18	...	1 Robert Stratford,[14] *Station Staff Officer, Dalhousie Depot*	25 June 58	2 Aug. 65
13	...	1 Augustus Wm. Whitworth,[14] *Inst. of Musk.* 25 Mar. 71	P12 June 63	P14 Sept. 67
13	...	1 Frederick Leigh Grundy	P 3 May 64	P 9 Nov. 67
12	...	2 James Lewis, *Adjutant* 27 Aug. 72	P 3 June 64	P30 Sept. 68
11	...	1 Richard Meredith[19]	P 9 May 65	P17 Mar. 69
11	...	2 Henry Deering Thomas	P 2 June 65	P29 May 69
9	...	1 Frank Longbourne	P27 July 66	P28 May 70
9	...	2 Neville Frederick Mansergh	P 4 Dec. 66	P27 Oct. 71
10	...	2 Gerald Hyde Charles Stracey[19]	P10 Nov. 65	28 Oct. 71
8	...	1 Edward Arthur Ball,[14] *Adjutant* 27 Apr. 75	P14 Sept. 67	28 Oct. 71
8	...	1 Arthur Mullaniffe O'Beirne	P27 Nov. 67	28 Oct. 71
7	...	1 Richard John Doyne	P30 Sept. 68	28 Oct. 71
7	...	2 Denman Croft Murray	23 Jan. 69	28 Oct. 71
7	...	1 Edward Henry Corse Scott	P10 Feb. 69	28 Oct. 71
6	...	1 Edw. Jno. Winnington-Ingram	P10 Nov. 69	28 Oct. 71
6	...	2 Willoughby E. Gordon Forbes	P10 Nov. 69	28 Oct. 71
6	...	1 Henry Blake Harward	P14 July 69	28 Oct. 71
7	...	1 St. George John Rathborne	P 2 Dec. 68	28 Oct. 71
3	...	1 Thomas George Lumsden	......	15 Jan. 73
2	...	1 Valens Congreve Tonnochy	......	9 Aug. 73
2	...	2 William Erskine Scott	......	9 Aug. 73
2	...	2 Gregory Haines	......	9 Aug. 73
2	...	2 Gilbert Moorcroft Yaldwyn	......	9 Aug. 73
2	...	2 Thomas Richard Francis Brabazon Hallowes	......	12 Nov. 73
1	...	2 John William Stevenson	......	2 Dec. 74

Full Pay	Half Pay	Sub Lieutenants.		Sub Lieut.
2	...	2 Morey Quayle Jones	......	12 Nov. 73
2	...	1 Henry Lushington Ramsay	......	28 Feb. 74
1	...	1 William Conrad Faithful	......	21 Sept. 74
1	...	1 Charles Edward Pollock	......	11 Feb. 75
1	...	Maurice Eyre	......	10 Sept. 75

Full Pay	Half Pay	
23	...	*Paymasters.*—2 John O'Connor,[22] 3 Nov. 57; *Q.M.* 11 Mar. 53; *Hon.Major*, 11 Mar. 68.
20	...	1 William Wastell,[23] 21 Dec. 60; *Ensign*, 30 Nov. 55; *Lt.* 26 Jan. 58; *Hon.Major*, 21 Dec. 70.
9	...	*Quarter Masters.*—1 George Beedle,[14] 10 July 66.
2	...	2 James Berryman Tippetts, 4 Oct. 73.
		Medical Officers.—2 *Surgeon Major* Francis John Shortt,[25] *Surgeon*, 29 Dec. 69.
		1 *Surgeon Major* Eugene Francis O'Leary, *Surgeon*, 30 Aug. 71.

[1] Lieut.General Crofton was appointed Persian Interpreter to the force under Brigadier General Litchfield in August 1832, and served with it throughout the arduous operations in Parkur, and against the tribes in the N.W. Desert, which ended in the taking of Balmeer. He was also employed at the defence of Aden against the Arabs in 1840-41; and commanded the expedition sent to the Red river, Prince Rupert's Land, *via* Hudson's Bay, in 1846, under instructions for the defence of the British settlements in the event of war with America for the Oregon territory. For this service he received the thanks of the Duke of Wellington and the Colonial Secretary.

[2] Colonel Osborne served with a party of Volunteers attached to the Scinde Camel Corps during Sir Charles Napier's campaign of 1845 against the mountain and desert tribes on the right bank of the Indus. Served on the Head Quarters Staff of the Azimghur Field Force during the campaign of 1858 in the N.W. Provinces of India, and was present at the action of 6th April before Azimghur and in the intrenchment of that place from 6th to 14th April, when besieged by Koer Sing's Force. Also at the assault of Jugdespore, actions at Jelowra 11th and 29th May, Metahi 24th May, and skirmishes in the Jugdespore Jungles (mentioned in despatches, Medal, and Brevet of Major). Commanded 1st Battalion 6th Regiment during the Hazara campaign of 1866, including the expedition against the Black Mountain tribes on the Punjaub Frontier (mentioned in despatches, Medal with Clasp, and *CB.*).

1st Batt. embarked for India, 7 Dec. 1867. Depôt, with 2nd Batt.
2nd Batt. returned from Jamaica, 3 May 1867.

Facings Blue.—*Agents*, Messrs. Cox and Co.—*Irish Agents*, *Sir* E. Borough, *Bt.* and Co.

K

Figure 3 Hart's Army Lists 1875 vol IV, p142 6th Foot

Between 1839 and 1915 a private rival to the Army List was published, initially by Lt Gen H G Hart. Hart's Army Lists are particularly valuable because they list promotions, together with brief descriptions of war service included for many officers.

This regiment here is the same regiment as used in the Army List example (figure 2). Hart's Army List gives much more information.

Of particular interest are the biographical details. The regimental colonel, Lt Gen John Crofton, for example is described as being 'appointed Persian Interpreter to the force under Brigadier-General Litchfield in August 1832 and served with it throughout the arduous operations in Parkur, and against the tribes in the N.W. Desert, which ended in the taking of Balmeer. He was employed at the defence of Aden against the Arabs in 1840-41; and commanded the expedition sent to the Red river, Prince Rupert's Land, via Hudson's Bay, in 1846 under instructions for the defence of the British settlements in the event of war with America for the Oregon territory. For this service he received the thanks of the Duke of Wellington and the Colonial Secretary.'

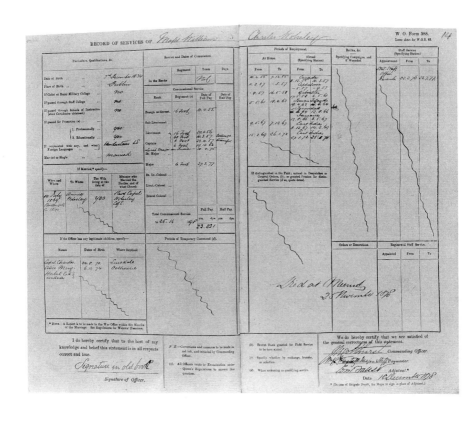

Figure 4 Officer's service record. WO 76/261 p14 Major William Charles Wolseley

This document summarizes the service of Major Wolseley in the Army until his death at Meerut during the Anglo-Afghan Wars of 1878-1881.

Of particular interest to the family historian are his place and date of birth and details of his wife Annie and 'legitimate children'

See also illustrations of his entries in the Army List (figure 2) and Hart's Army List (figure 3)

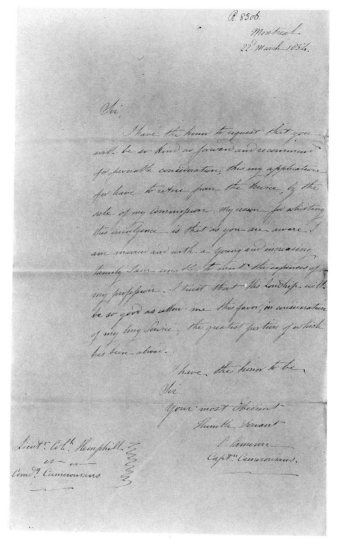

Figure 5 Commander in chief memoranda. WO 31/1048 bundle for 22 March 1854 Captain Charles Cameron

These memoranda refer to the purchase and sale of commissions by officers. They are kept in bundles wrapped in red tape. Each bundle contains a week's worth of memoranda. It is possible to discover which bundle an officer is likely to appear from *Hart's Army Lists*. These records can be difficult to use as they consist of very tightly folded loose papers.

The example here is for the retirement of Captain Charles Cameron of the 26th Regiment by means of the sale of his commission. He gives his reason for leaving the army 'I am married and with a large and increasing family I am unable to meet the expenses of my profession.'

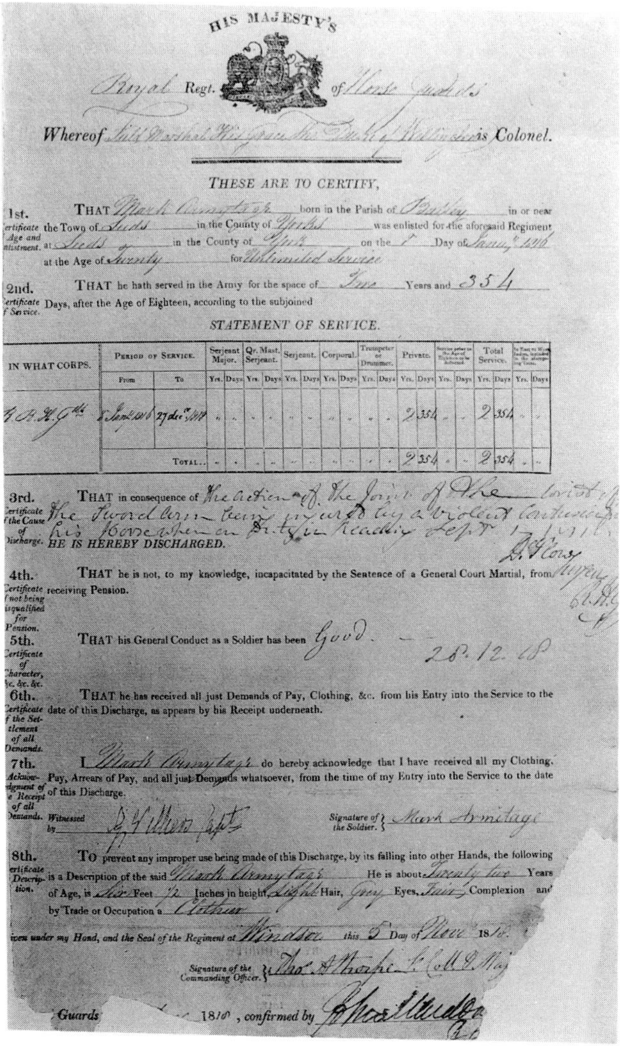

Figure 6 Soldiers' documents WO 97/1 pt 1 Mark Armytage

Soldiers' documents are the most important record for family historians tracing other ranks. The documents survive only for men who received a pension. Soldiers' documents begin in 1760 and end in 1913, although there are very few before the 1790s. As the nineteenth century progressed they become much more detailed.

The figure shows the document for Mark Armytage, a clothier of Leeds, who served in the Horse Guards and was discharged in 1818 aged about 22. He had served with the regiment nearly three years until he was thrown from his horse. The document records that Armytage was discharged in consequence of 'the action of the join of the wrist of the sword arm being injured by a violent contusion from his horse when on duty in Reading depot.'

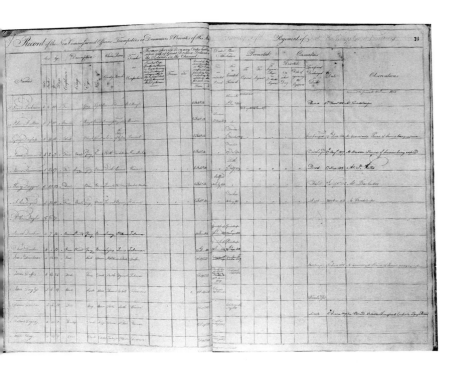

Figure 7 WO 25/351 f29v, 30r Description book for the 28th Foot (King's Own Borderers)

Description books describe each soldier, his place of birth, trade, service and place of enlistment, together with some idea of his career and when he died or was discharged.

This example is for the 28th Foot who were serving in the West Indies towards the end of the Napoleonic Wars. Take for example the entry on the page for George Douglass. He is listed as being 18 at time of enlistment and a servant by trade. Douglass was discharged in Guadeloupe on 19 June 1816, his time of service expired.

What makes George Douglass unusual is that he is described as having a black complexion and being born in Ceylon. Presumably he was either of African or Asian descent.

There were a number of negroes serving in the army at this time, mainly with the West India Regiment, but sometimes with other regiments. It would be interesting to know more about Douglass' background and what happened to him when he left the army.

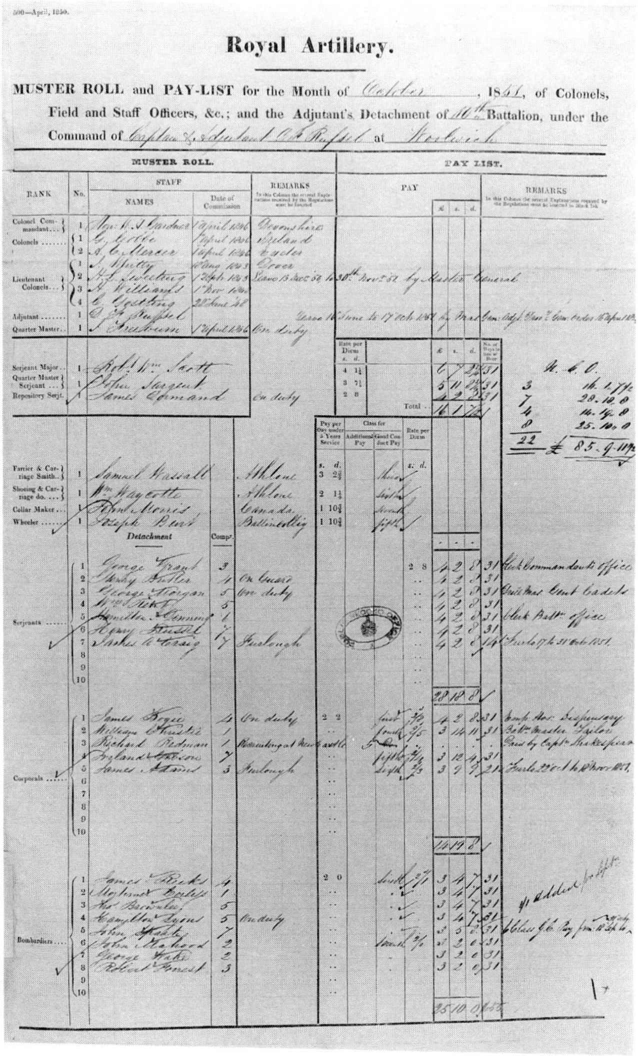

500—April, 1850.

Royal Artillery.

MUSTER ROLL and PAY-LIST for the Month of October, 1851, of Colonels, Field and Staff Officers, &c.; and the Adjutant's Detachment of 10th Battalion, under the Command of Captain & Adjutant C. F. Russel at Woolwich

MUSTER ROLL. — PAY LIST.

Rank	No.	Names	Remarks
Colonel Commandant	1	Major Genl. A. Gardner	Devonshire
Colonels	1	G. Cobbe	Ireland
	2	A. C. Mercer	Exeter
Lieutenant Colonels	1	J. Whitty	Dover
	2	H. L. Sweeting	Leave 13 Decr 50 to 30th Novr 51 by Master General
	3	H. Williams	
	4	C. Gostling	
Adjutant	1	C. F. Russel	
Quarter Master	1	J. Freeburn	On duty
Serjeant Major	1	Robt. Wm. Scott	
Quarter Master Serjeant	1	John Sargent	
Repository Serjt.	1	James Ormand	On duty
Farrier & Carriage Smith	1	Samuel Hassall	Athlone
Shoeing & Carriage do.	1	Wm. Waycotte	Athlone
Collar Maker	1	Robert Morris	Canada
Wheeler	1	Joseph Burt	Ballincollig
Serjeants	1	George Grant	Clerk Commandant's Office
	2	Henry Butler	On Guard
	3	George Morgan	On duty
Corporals	1	James Bogie	On duty; Hosp. Dispensary
	2	William Christie	Bdr. master Tailor
	3	Richard Redman	Recruiting at Newcastle
	5	James Adams	Furlough

Figure 8 Muster roll WO 10/2086 October 1851 Adjutant's detachment, 10th Battalion, Royal Artillery stationed at Woolwich

Muster rolls were designed to record the payment of pay and other allowances to soldier month by month. They also include other details, for example: when men joined, left or died; where men served; and deductions from pay as punishment

This example is for the Adjutant's detachment, 10th Battalion, Royal Artillery which was stationed at Woolwich in October 1851. It records for example that Lt Col Sweeting was on leave, that Farrier Samuel Hassall was at Athlone presumably on detached duty, and that Corporal Richard Redman was recruiting at Newcastle. Corporal James Bogie it was noted was employed in the hospital dispensary.

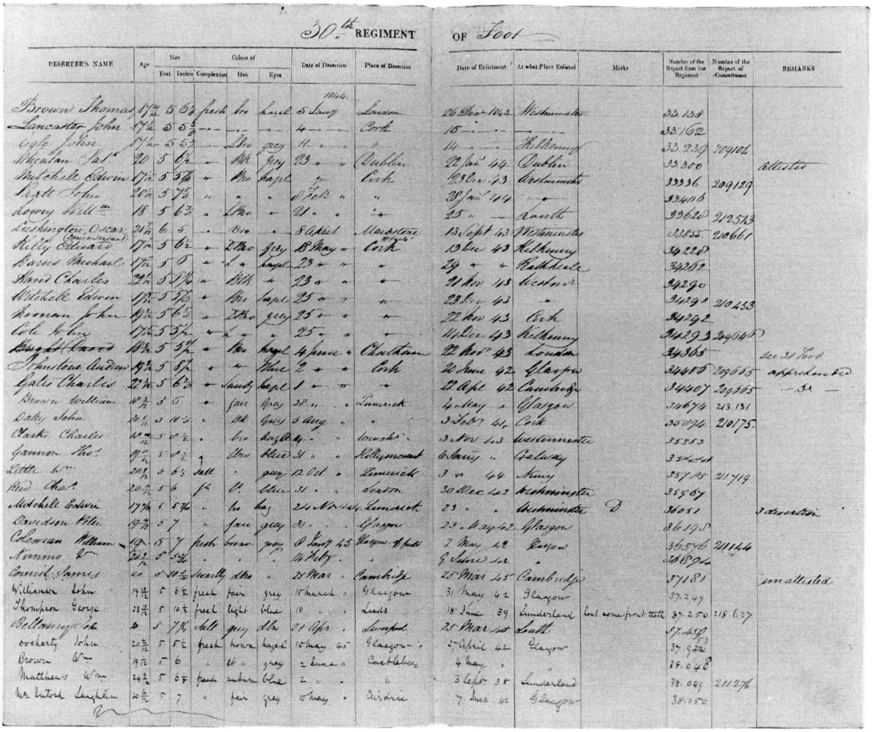

Figure 9 Deserters. WO 25/2925 30th Foot, 1844

Desertion from the army was by no means uncommon in the nineteenth century. These pages list deserters from the 30th Foot in 1844 and 1845. Considerable detail is given about each deserter.

Take, for example, the first entry on the page. Thomas Brown is aged $17\frac{1}{2}$. He is 5 foot $6\frac{1}{8}$ inches tall, with a fresh complexion, brown hair and hazel eyes. He deserted in London on 5 January 1844, having enlisted barely a week before in Westminster on Boxing Day 1843.

Thomas Brown wasn't caught, although several other men in the register deserted several times and were subsequently apprehended.

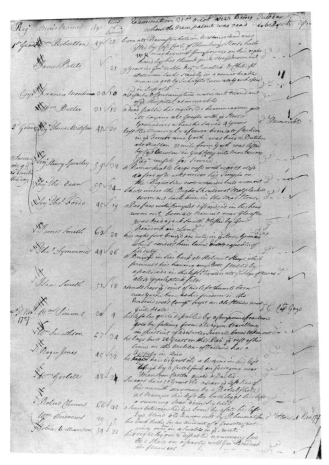

Figure 10 Admission books, Royal Hospital Chelsea WO 116/2 31 October 1727

Before men could be admitted for an out-pension from the Royal Hospital Chelsea they had to be examined by a doctor. The admission books cover the period 1715-1913.

Later books give a summary of army service, the 'complaint', place of birth and physical description. Earlier books are not as well structured.

This book dates from 1727 and is full of fascinating descriptions of men's careers and their complaints.

Take for example Sergeant Thomas Wilson (fifth entry down), age 41 with twenty years service in the 2nd Guards, who 'left his memory by a fever. Born at Stockton in the forrest near York, was bred a butcher at Malton 13 miles from York, was lifted by Capt Dawson in York Citty into [?Montances] Regt. Unfit for service.' He was reported, that is awarded a pension

Another example is Sergeant Henry Spratley (sixth entry on page), age 59 with 38 years service, who has 'a remarkable large nose with warts alife, alsort of warts under his temple on the right side. Note wounded but worn out.' He too received a pension.

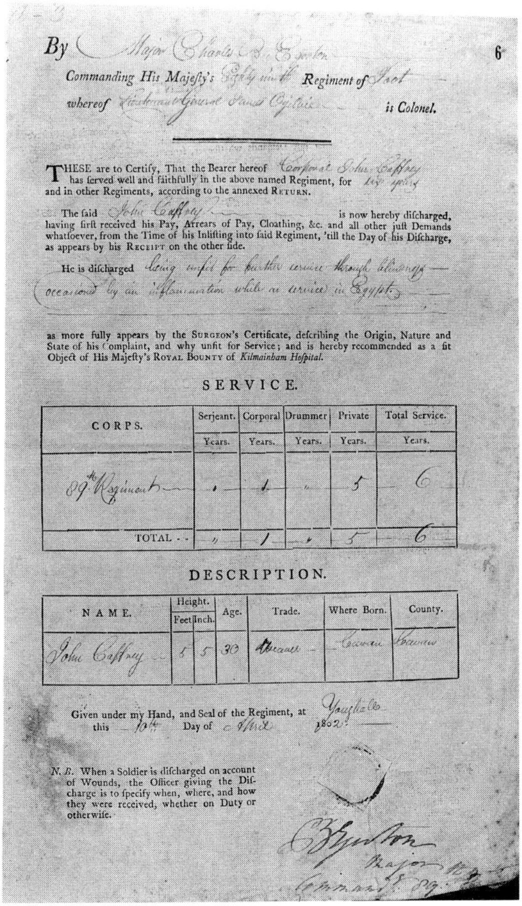

By Major Charles B. Egerton 6

Commanding His Majesty's Eighty ninth *Regiment of* Foot

whereof Lieutenant General Lord Ogilvie *is Colonel.*

THESE are to Certify, That the Bearer hereof Corporal John Caffrey has served well and faithfully in the above named Regiment, for six years and in other Regiments, according to the annexed RETURN.

The said John Caffrey is now hereby discharged, having first received his Pay, Arrears of Pay, Cloathing, &c. and all other just Demands whatsoever, from the Time of his Inlisting into said Regiment, 'till the Day of his Discharge, as appears by his RECEIPT on the other side.

He is discharged being unfit for further service through blindness occasioned by an inflammation while on service in Egypt

as more fully appears by the SURGEON's Certificate, describing the Origin, Nature and State of his Complaint, and why unfit for Service; and is hereby recommended as a fit Object of His Majesty's ROYAL BOUNTY of *Kilmainham Hospital.*

SERVICE.

CORPS.	Serjeant.	Corporal	Drummer	Private	Total Service.
	Years.	Years.	Years.	Years.	Years.
89th Regiment	„	1	„	5	6
TOTAL - -	„	1	„	5	6

DESCRIPTION.

NAME.	Height. Feet	Height. Inch.	Age.	Trade.	Where Born.	County.
John Caffrey	5	5	30	Weaver	Clare	Clare

Given under my Hand, and Seal of the Regiment, at Youghalle this 10th Day of April 1802.

N. B. When a Soldier is discharged on account of Wounds, the Officer giving the Discharge is to specify when, where, and how they were received, whether on Duty or otherwise.

C B Egerton
Major
Command 89

Figure 11 Admission books, Royal Hospital Kilmainham. WO 119/1 f6 Corporal John Caffrey

The Royal Hospital Kilmainham operated in Ireland in a similar to that in which the Royal Hospital Chelsea did in Britain. It was responsible for the award of pensions and as a result its records can be of great use for tracing Irish ancestors.

The example here is for Corporal John Caffrey of the 89th Foot who became blind while serving in Egypt. The discharge document indicates that he was discharged aged 30 in 1802. By trade John Caffrey was a weaver in County Clare. He had served for six years.

Attached to the document is an accompanying appeal for a pension written ten years later in 1812, addressed to the earl of Harrington, master of Kilmainham hospital. In it he writes:

That mem[oralist] was sent home to the Dublin Hospital and after some time turned out incurable. That mem[oralist] has only 1s 2d per day and is creditably informed that some private[s] have that has not gone thro[ugh] so long arduous service as mem[oralist] has served. That mem[oralist] has a wife & large helpless family unable to earn their bread or any relations on whom they might now rely.

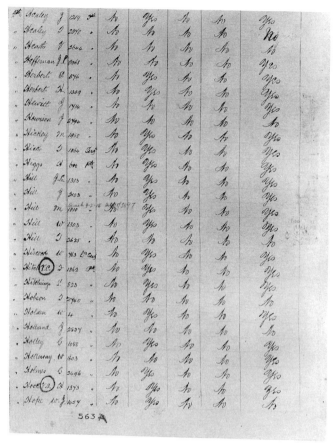

Figure 12 Medal roll. WO 100/46 pt 3 f 172 v,

Award of South African War Medal to Privates Hitch and Hook, 24th Regiment

This example has columns, reading from left to right, for:
Rank; name; rank and regimental number at time medal awarded; Whether in possession of the medal for previous wars; Whether engaged against the Gaikas and other Kaffir tribes; Whether engaged against Pokwane 1878; whether engaged against the Griquas 1878; whether engaged against the Zulus 1879

Other entries in the medal roll show whether the applicant had engaged against Sekunini; whether engaged against Moiroris stronghold; entitled to clasp; other remarks: serving with regiment or depot, dead, discharged deserted etc.

Privates Frederick Hitch and Alfred Henry Hook received the Victoria Cross for their gallantry at Rorke's Drift in 1879. See also figure 13. The medal roll contains a press cutting, dating from 1929, saying that Private Hitch's medal had been sold for £35.

Note also that Private Hope, the name below that of Alfred Hook received no medal because he had deserted.

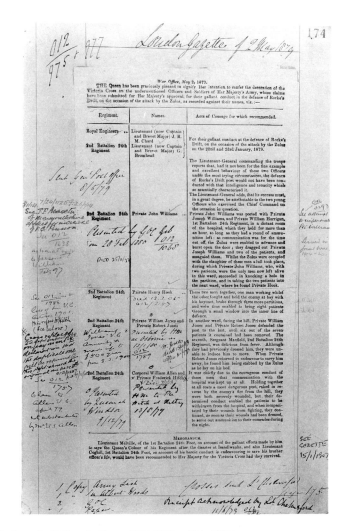

Figure 13 Award of Victoria Cross WO 98/4 p174 1879

The Victoria Cross was instituted in 1856 and quickly became the most prestigious of British medals for gallantry.

The example here refers to Victoria Crosses awarded for the action at Rorke's Drift when a few men of the 24th Regiment (later the South Wales Borderers) defended a mission station against attack from Zulu warriors.

The page is an extract from the *London Gazette* of 2 May 1879, with manuscript additions indicating when the medal was awarded and the future career of the men. It is noted here that Private John Williams served in the First World War and died in 1932. He must have been one of the very few veterans of the Zulu War who did so. There is also a note in the margin of an attempt to impersonate Private Williams.

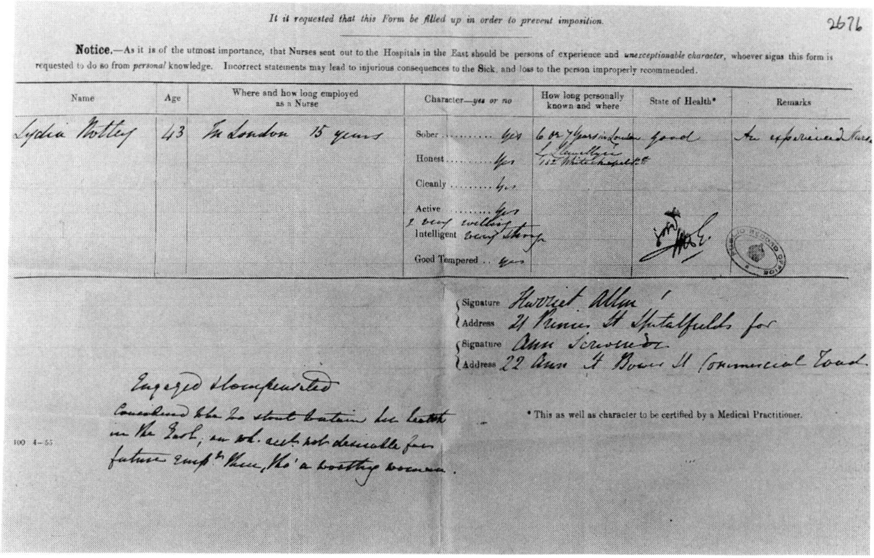

It is requested that this Form be filled up in order to prevent imposition. 2676

Notice.—As it is of the utmost importance, that Nurses sent out to the Hospitals in the East should be persons of experience and *unexceptionable character*, whoever signs this form is requested to do so from *personal* knowledge. Incorrect statements may lead to injurious consequences to the Sick, and loss to the person improperly recommended.

Name	Age	Where and how long employed as a Nurse	Character—*yes or no*	How long personally known and where	State of Health*	Remarks
Lydia Notley	43	In London 15 years	Sober ... yes Honest ... yes Cleanly ... yes Active ... yes Intelligent ... very strong Good Tempered ... yes	6 or 7 years in London L. Llewellyn 152 Whitechapel Rd	good	An experienced Nurse

Signature Harriet Allen
Address 21 Princes St Spitalfields for
Signature Ann Scrivener
Address 22 Ann St Bower St Commercial Road

Engaged & compensated
Considered to be too stout to sustain her health in the East; on wh. acct not desirable for future empt there, tho' a worthy woman.

* This as well as character to be certified by a Medical Practitioner.

100 4–55

Figure 14 Nurses' testimonial Crimean War WO 25/264 No 2676 Lydia Notley

In 1855 the first female nurses were recruited for service in the Crimea. Many thousands of women applied and their applications are held by the PRO. They are usually handwritten. This example is one of the few forms which survive.

Miss Notley however was not destined to nurse soldiers. The note in the bottom left hand corner reads:

Engaged & compensated. Considered to be too stout [to] sustain her health in the East; on wh[ich] ac[ount]t not desirable for future emp[loyment] there, tho[ugh] a worthy woman.

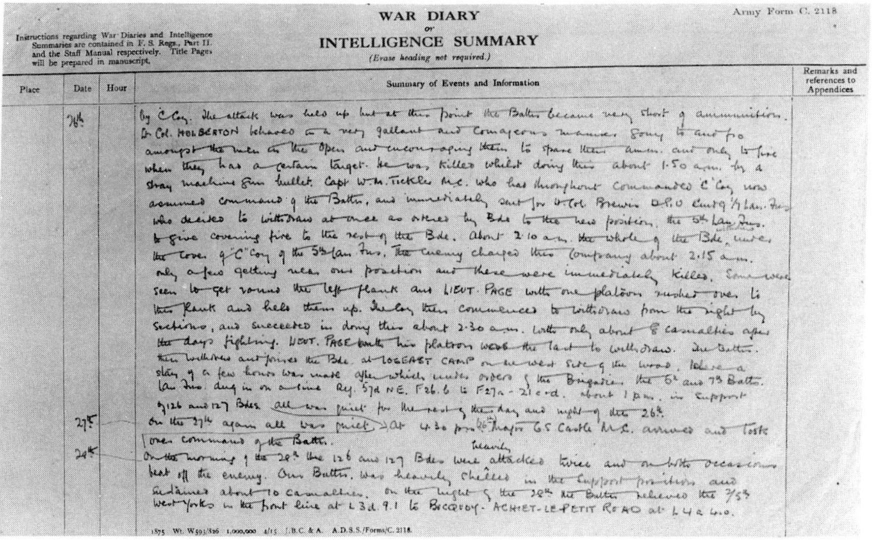

WAR DIARY
or
INTELLIGENCE SUMMARY
(Erase heading not required.)

Army Form C. 2118

Instructions regarding War Diaries and Intelligence Summaries are contained in F. S. Regs., Part II. and the Staff Manual respectively. Title Pages will be prepared in manuscript.

Place	Date	Hour	Summary of Events and Information	Remarks and references to Appendices
	26th		by "C" Coy. The attack was held up but at this point the Battn became very short of ammunition. Lt Col. HOLBERTON behaved in a very gallant and courageous manner going to and fro amongst the men in the open and encouraging them to spare their amm. and only to fire when they had a certain target. he was killed whilst doing this about 1.50 a.m. by a stray machine gun bullet. Capt W. M. Tickler M.C. who had throughout commanded "C" Coy now assumed command of the Battn, and immediately sent for Lt Col. Brewis D.S.O. Cmdg 1/7 Lan. Fus who decided to withdraw at once as ordered by Bde to the new position, the 5th Lan. Fus. to give covering fire to the rest of the Bde. About 2.10 a.m. the whole of the Bde withdrew under the cover of "C" Coy of the 5th Lan. Fus. The enemy charged this Company about 2.15 a.m. only a few getting near our position and these were immediately killed. Some were seen to get round the left flank and LIEUT. PAGE with one platoon rushed over to this flank and held them up. The Coy then commenced to withdraw from the right by sections, and succeeded in doing this about 2.30 a.m. with only about 8 casualties after the days fighting. LIEUT. PAGE with his platoon were the last to withdraw. The Battn. then withdrew and joined the Bde. at LOGEAST CAMP on the west side of the wood, where a stay of a few hours was made after which under orders of the Brigadier the 5th and 7th Battn. Lan. Fus. dug in on a line Ref. 57d NE. F26.b to F27a - 21 c+d. about 1 p.m. in support of 126 and 127 Bdes. all was quiet for the rest of the day and night of the 26th.	
	27th		On the 27th again all was quiet. At 4.30 pm (26th) Major G.S. Castle M.C. arrived and took over command of the Battn.	
	28th		On the morning of the 28th the 126 and 127 Bdes were heavily attacked twice and on both occasions beat off the enemy. Our Battn. was heavily shelled in the support positions and sustained about 10 casualties. On the night of the 28th the Battn relieved the 7/5th West Yorks in the front line at L 3d. 9.1 to BUCQUOY - ACHIET-LE-PETIT ROAD at L 4 a 4.0.	

1875 Wt. W593/826 1,000,000 4/15 J.B.C. & A. A.D.S.S./Forms/C. 2118.

Figure 15 War diaries WO 95/2654 26 March 1918 1/5th Battalion, Lancashire Fusiliers

War diaries have been kept by all British Army units engaged in combat since 1907. They contain a detailed day by day account of unit activities. War diaries were designed to be used by the General Staff to learn strategic lessons from wars. They have also been used by military historians to write the history of battles.

They are also of great value to the family historian as they record activities day by day. Unfortunately what ordinary soldiers did is rarely recorded, this is particularly true of diaries from the First World War.

This example is for the 1/5th Battalion, Lancashire Fusiliers, 26 March 1918. At the time the battalion was at Gomiecourt Ridge in Northern France stemming the German push towards Paris.

At 1.50 am the diarist noted 'Lt Col Holberton behaved in a very gallant and courageous manner going to and fro amongst the men on the open and encouraging them to spare their am[munition] and only to fire when they have a certain target. He was killed whilst doing this about 1.50am by a stray bullet...'

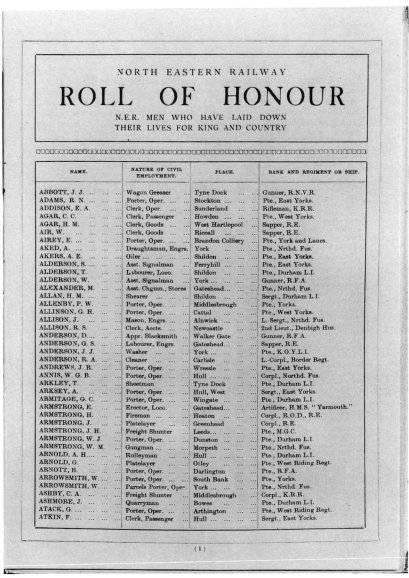

NORTH EASTERN RAILWAY

ROLL OF HONOUR

N.E.R. MEN WHO HAVE LAID DOWN
THEIR LIVES FOR KING AND COUNTRY

NAME.	NATURE OF CIVIL EMPLOYMENT.	PLACE.	RANK AND REGIMENT OR SHIP.
ABBOTT, J. J.	Wagon Greaser	Tyne Dock	Gunner, R.N.V.R.
ADAMS, R. N.	Porter, Oper.	Stockton	Pte., East Yorks.
ADDISON, E. A.	Clerk, Oper.	Sunderland	Rifleman, K.R.R.
AGAR, C. C.	Clerk, Passenger	Howden	Pte., West Yorks.
AGAR, H. M.	Clerk, Goods	West Hartlepool	Sapper, R.E.
AIR, W.	Clerk, Goods	Riccall	Sapper, R.E.
AIREY, E.	Porter, Oper.	Brandon Colliery	Pte., York and Lancs.
AKED, A.	Draughtsman, Engrs.	York	Pte., Nrthd. Fus.
AKERS, A. E.	Oiler	Shildon	Pte., East Yorks.
ALDERSON, S.	Asst. Signalman	Ferryhill	Pte., East Yorks.
ALDERSON, T.	Labourer, Loco.	Shildon	Pte., Durham L.I.
ALDERSON, W.	Asst. Signalman	York	Gunner, R.F.A.
ALEXANDER, M.	Asst. Chgmn., Stores	Gateshead	Pte., Nrthd. Fus.
ALLAN, H. M.	Shearer	Shildon	Sergt., Durham L.I.
ALLENBY, P. W.	Porter, Oper.	Middlesbrough	Pte., Yorks.
ALLINSON, G. H.	Porter, Oper.	Cattal	Pte., West Yorks.
ALLISON, J.	Mason, Engrs.	Alnwick	L.-Sergt., Nrthd. Fus.
ALLISON, R. S.	Clerk, Accts.	Newcastle	2nd Lieut., Denbigh Hus.
ANDERSON, D.	Appr. Blacksmith	Walker Gate	Gunner, R.F.A.
ANDERSON, G. S.	Labourer, Engrs.	Gateshead	Sapper, R.E.
ANDERSON, J. J.	Washer	York	Pte., K.O.Y.L.I.
ANDERSON, R. A.	Cleaner	Carlisle	L.-Corpl., Border Regt.
ANDREWS, J. R.	Porter, Oper.	Wressle	Pte., East Yorks.
ANNIS, W. G. B.	Porter, Oper.	Hull	Corpl., Nrthd. Fus.
ARKLEY, T.	Sheetman	Tyne Dock	Pte., Durham L.I.
ARKSEY, A.	Porter, Oper.	Hull, West	Sergt., East Yorks.
ARMITAGE, G. C.	Porter, Oper.	Wingate	Pte., Durham L.I.
ARMSTRONG, E.	Erector, Loco.	Gateshead	Artificer, H.M.S. " Yarmouth."
ARMSTRONG, H.	Fireman	Heaton	Corpl., R.O.D., R.E.
ARMSTRONG, J.	Platelayer	Greenhead	Corpl., R.E.
ARMSTRONG, J. H.	Freight Shunter	Leeds	Pte., M.G.C.
ARMSTRONG, W. J.	Porter, Oper.	Dunston	Pte., Durham L.I.
ARMSTRONG, W. M.	Gangman	Morpeth	Pte., Nrthd. Fus.
ARNOLD, A. H.	Rulleyman	Hull	Pte., Durham L.I.
ARNOLD, G.	Platelayer	Otley	Pte., West Riding Regt.
ARNOTT, B.	Porter, Oper.	Darlington	Pte., R.F.A.
ARROWSMITH, W.	Porter, Oper.	South Bank	Pte., Yorks.
ARROWSMITH, W.	Parcels Porter, Oper.	York	Pte., Nrthd. Fus.
ASHBY, C. A.	Freight Shunter	Middlesbrough	Corpl., K.R.R.
ASHMORE, J.	Quarryman	Bowes	Pte., Durham L.I.
ATACK, G.	Porter, Oper.	Arthington	Pte., West Riding Regt.
ATKIN, F.	Clerk, Passenger	Hull	Sergt., East Yorks.

(1)

Figure 16 Rolls of honour, First World War. RAIL 527/993 North Eastern Railway

At the end of the First World War many companies and other institutions compiled lists, or rolls of honour, of their employees who either died or served with the forces during the war.

A number of these rolls are at the PRO in the records of the pre-nationalization railway companies.

The example lists some of the men of the North Eastern Railway who died during the war.

INDEX

1914 Star 48

1914-1915 Star 48

A

Abyssinia
  War diaries 53

Admission books
  Colonial and dominion forces 35
  In-pensions 23
  Out-pensions 22
  Royal Artillery 26

Algeria
  War diaries 51

American War of Independence
  Hessian troops 38
  Loyalist troops 36
  Prisoners of war 45

Appointments
  Barrackmasters 40,44
  Board of Ordnance 44
  Commissariat Department 41
  Nurses 43
  Officers 12
  Royal Artillery 25
  Royal Engineers 26

Army
  Organization 2,3

Army Air Corps
  Operation record books 53

Army Hospital Corps 43

Army Lists 10, 11, 12, 15, 17, 49, 66

Army Medical Department 42

Army Nursing Service 43

Army Ordnance Corps 44

Army Purchase Commission 12,13

Army Register Books 61

Artillery, see Royal Artillery

Attestation and discharge papers 18

Attestation forms
  Militia 28

Australia
  Australian War Memorial holdings 37
  Courts martial 33
  Korean War 37
  Second World War 36
  Service records 37
  Settlement of former soldiers 24

Austria
  Quarterly Historical Reports 53

Auxiliary Territorial Service 52

B

Baptism records
  Foreign troops 38
  General Register Office holdings 61
  Loyalist 36
  Militia 28
  Officers 6, 12
  Registers 6
  Royal Horse Artillery 6,26
  Royal Hospital Chelsea 6

Barrackmasters 40,44

Battalions
  Organization 4, 5

Belgium
  First World War 47,48,49
  War diaries 52

Birth records
  Foreign troops 38, 39
  General Register Office holdings 6, 17, 34, 61
  General Register Office, Dublin holdings 62
  General Register Office for Scotland holdings 62
  Loyalist 36
  Militia 28
  Officers 6, 15, 16
  Oriental and India Office Collections holdings 34, 60

Other ranks 19, 22, 24
Registers 6, 61
Royal Artillery 25
Royal Engineers 45

Board of Ordnance 40, 44
Medical Department 43

British Army of the Rhine
Quarterly Historical Reports 53

British German Legion 39

British War Medal 48

Burial records
General Register Office holdings 61
Officers 6
Registers 6, 61
Royal Hospital Chelsea 6

Burma
Casualty rolls 7
War diaries 52

Buttervant (Ireland)
Registers of births 6

C

Camp followers 21

Canada
Courts martial 33
First World War 36, 37
Half pay 35
Korean War 37
Loyalists 36
Militia 35
Service records 37, 38
Soldiers' documents 34
South African War (1899-1902) 36

Canterbury garrison (Kent)
Burial registers6

Cape Mounted Rifles 35

Caribbean
Quarterly Historical Reports 53

Casualty returns 7
Battle of Waterloo 14
Colonial and dominion forces 35, 36
First World War 36, 48, 50, 60

Foreign troops 36, 39
Officers 7
Other ranks 4, 7, 8, 51
Royal Artillery 26
Royal Flying Corps 50
Second World War 51, 60, 61
South African War
(1899-1902) 7, 36, 61
Twentieth century 60
Veterans 42
see also Death Records

Cavaliers 9
Cavalry regiments
Muster rolls 20, 34
Organization 4

Census records 8

Central Mediterranean Forces
Quarterly Historical Reports 53
War diaries 51

Ceylon Regiment 35

Ceylon Rifles 35

Changi (Singapore)
Prisoner of War camp 33

Chaplains 40, 41

Chasseurs Britanniques 38

Chelsea Pensioners 23, 29
see also Royal Hospital Chelsea

China
Casualty rolls 7

Civilian employees 41
Board of Ordnance 44
Commissariat 41
Ordnance Survey 44

Colonial and dominion forces
Casualty returns 35, 36
Courts martial 33
First World War 49
Korean War 37
Medals 30
Militia 28, 35, 36
Muster rolls 20, 35, 36
Officers 35, 36
Other ranks 34, 35, 36, 37

Pensions 35
Prisoners of War 45, 46
Second World War 36, 51
Soldiers' documents 34

Commissariat Department 41

Commissions 9, 11, 12, 13, 14, 15
Purchase 12, 13
Royal Artillery 25
Royal Engineers 26
Sale 12, 14, 15

Companion of the Bath (CB) 31

Compassionate Fund 16

Compassionate List 16

Connaught Rangers 60

Connecticut
Militia units 36

Conscientious objectors 50

Courts martial
Colonial and dominion forces 33
First World War 33
Ireland 32
Officers 32
Other ranks 32
Second World War 33

Crimean War
Casualty returns 7
Foreign troops in British pay 39
Medals 30, 31
Muster rolls 20
Nurses 43
Prisoners of war 45

D

Death records
First World War 48, 61
Foreign troops 38
General Register Office
holdings 6, 34, 61
General Register Office,
Dublin holdings 62
General Register Office,
for Scotland holdings 62
Loyalist 36
Militia 28

Officers 6, 15, 16, 48
Oriental and India Office
Collections holdings 34, 60
Other ranks 18, 20, 23
Royal Artillery 7, 25
Royal Engineers 7, 27, 44, 45
Sappers and Miners 27
Second World War 61

Description books 17, 19, 20, 71
Royal Artillery 26
Royal Horse Artillery 26
Sappers and miners 27

Deserters 7, 20, 21, 26, 33, 73

Dillon's Regiment 38

Discharges 18, 19

Distinguished Conduct Medal
(DCM) 30, 31, 49

Distinguished Service Order (DSO) 31

Dover Castle (Kent)
Registers of births 6

Drouly's Annuities 16

Duke of York's Royal Military School 46

E

East Africa
Quarterly Historical Reports 53

East India Company Army **see** India

Egypt
Casualty rolls 7
Second World War 51
War diaries 53

Emigration 24, 39

Engineers **see** Royal Engineers

English Civil War 9

Enrolled Pensioners 42

F

Far East

Quarterly Historical Reports 53

Fencibles
    Muster books 28

Fermoy (Ireland)
    Registers of births 6

First World War
    Belgium 48, 49
    Casualty returns 7, 36, 48, 50, 60
    Colonial and dominion forces 49
    Courts martial 33
    Death records 48, 61
    France 48, 49, 50
    Indian Army 34
    Italy 49
    Medals 30, 31, 48, 49
    Medical records 48
    Mesopotamia 49
    Military Service Tribunals 50
    Nurses 43, 44, 50
    Palestine 49
    Pensions 48
    Prisoners of war 45
    Rolls of honour 48
    Russia 49
    Salonika 49
    Service records 47
    War diaries 49, 79
    Women 50

Foreign troops in British pay
    French 38
    German 37, 38, 39
    Greek 38
    Half pay 39
    Hessian 38
    Italian 38, 39
    Muster rolls 20, 39
    Officers 39
    Polish 39. 40
    Swiss 38, 39

Foreign Veterans Battalion 39

France
    First World War 48, 49, 50
    Second World War 51, 52

French Emigrant Engineers
    and Artillery 38

G

Garrison Battalions 42

George Cross (GC) 59

Germany
    British Army of the Rhine 53
    Hessian Troops in British pay 38
    Post First World War armies of
      occupation 49
    Second World War 52
    Troops in British pay 37, 38, 39

GHQ Liaison Regiment 51

Gibraltar
    Quarterly Historical Reports 53

Giessen (Germany)
    Prisoners of war 45

Gloucester Regiment 14

Gosport (Hants)
    Discharge depot 34

Gradation lists 10, 11

Greece
    Second World War 51
    Troops in British pay 38

Guards regiments
    Muster rolls 20

Gun Lascars 35

H

Half pay 14, 15, 25, 35
    Commissariat 41
    Foreign troops 39
    Royal Engineers 27

Hanover
    Troops in British pay 38

Hart's Army Lists 11, 12, 67

Holland
    War diaries 52

Home Forces
    First World War 49
    Quarterly Historical Reports 53
    Second World War 51

Home Guard 52

I

Identifying a regiment 17, 18

Imperial Yeomanry 36

India
    Courts martial 32
    East India Company Army 33
    First World War 34
    Indian Army 33, 34, 60
    National Army Museum
        holdings 34, 60
    Oriental and India Office
        Collection holdings 33, 34, 60
    Pensions 33
    Second World War 34, 52
    War diaries 53

In-pensions **see** Pensions

Inspection returns 14

Invalids 41, 42
    Royal Corps of 42

Ireland
    British Army regiments 60
    Courts martial 32
    Easter rising 53
    Militia 28
    Pensions 19, 22, 23
    see also Royal Hospital Kilmainham

Italy
    First World War 49
    Second World War 51
    Troops in British pay 38, 39

J

Jewish chaplains 40

K

King's African Rifles 36

King's German Legion 38, 39

King's Own Yorkshire Light Infantry 6

King's South Africa Medal 30, 43

Korean War
    Commonwealth Division 37
    Prisoners of War 46

War diaries 37, 53

Kurdistan (Iraq)
    Campaign medal 30

L

Ladysmith (South Africa) 14

Leinster Regiment 60

Libya
    Second World War 51

Location of units 4, 5, 10, 18

Long Service and Good Conduct Medal
    30

Lydenburg (South Africa) 14

M

Madagascar
    Second World War 51

Malaya
    War diaries 52

Malta
    Quarterly Historical Reports 53

Marine Officers **see** Royal Marines

Marriage records
    Foreign troops 38
    General Register Office
        holdings 6, 34, 61
    General Register Office,
        Dublin holdings 62
    General Register Office for Scotland
        holdings 62
    Loyalist 36
    Officers 6, 13, 16
    Oriental and India Office
        Collections holdings 34, 60
    Other ranks 20
    Registers 6, 61
    Royal Artillery 6, 25
    Royal Engineers 27, 45
    Royal Horse Artillery 6, 26
    Royal Hospital Chelsea 6

Massachusetts
    Militia units 36

Medals and awards
   Campaign medals 29, 30, 76
   Citations 31, 49, 52
   Colonial campaigns 30
   First World War 3, 48, 49
   Gallantry medals 30, 31
   Long service and good conduct 30
   Peninsular War 30
   Royal Army Medical Corps 43
   Second World War 52
   see also individual medals and awards

Medical services
   War diaries 51

Medical staff
   Officers 11, 42, 43
   Service records 42, 43
   see also Nurses

Mentions in despatches 31, 49

Meritorious Service Medal 30, 49

Mesopotamia
   First World War 49

Meuron's Regiment 38

Middle East
   Quarterly Historial Reports 53
   War diaries 51

Military General Service Medal 29, 30

Military Medal (MM) 48, 49

Military Surveyors and Draughtsmen,
   Royal Corps of 46

Military Train 41

Militia
   Baptism and birth records 28
   Canadian 35
   Chelsea pensioners 29
   Colonial and dominion 28, 35, 36
   Death records 28
   Local record office holdings 59
   Medals 30
   Muster rolls 8, 9, 20, 28
   Officers 28, 29
   Other ranks 28, 29
   Soldiers' documents 29

Monthly returns 4, 5

Muster rolls 20, 24
   Cavalry regiments 20
   Chelsea Pensioners 2
   Colonial and dominion forces 20,
      35, 36
   Crimean War 20
   Foreign troops 20, 38, 39
   Guards regiments 20
   India 34
   Militia 8, 9, 20, 28
   Royal Artillery 20, 25
   Royal Engineers 20, 27
   Royal Flying Corps 50
   Scutari Depot 20
   Veterans battalions 42

N

Napoleonic wars
   Casualties 7
   French troops in British pay 38
   Medals 30
   Militia 29
   Prisoners of War 45

Natal
   Volunteer units 36

National Aid Society 43

Netley (Hants)
   Victoria Hospital 34, 43
New Hampshire
   Militia units 36

New Zealand
   Casualty returns 7
   Medals 30
   National Archives of
      New Zealand holdings 37
   Service records 37
   Settlement of former soldiers 24, 37

Next of kin 7, 18

Niger and West Africa Force 36

North America
   Provincial volunteer forces 36

North Carolina
   Loyalist militia 36

Norway
  War diaries 51

Nubia (Sudan)
  Campaign medals 30

Nurses 43, 44, 50
  First World War 43, 49, 50
  Second World War 44, 52
  see also Medical staff

O

Officers
  Appointments 12
  Baptism records 6, 12
  Birth records 6, 15, 16
  Burial records 6
  Casualty returns 7
  Children 13, 16
  Colonial and dominion forces 35, 36
  Commissariat 41
  Commissions 12, 13
  Courts martial 32
  Death records 6, 15, 16, 48
  Dependants' allowances 16
  First World War 47
  Foreign troops in British pay 38, 39
  Garrison battalions 42
  Half pay 14, 15, 36
  India 13, 33, 34
  Marriage records 6, 13, 16
  Medical staff 11, 42, 43
  Militia 28, 29
  Pensions 15, 16, 48
  Purchase and sale of
    commissions 12
  Ranks 9, 10, 55
  Royal Artillery 11, 25
  Royal Engineers 11, 26, 27, 44
  Royal Garrison Regiment 14, 42
  Service records 10, 11, 13, 14, 17,
    28, 34, 68, 69
  Submissions to the sovereign 12
  Unattached pay 14
  Widows 16, 39

Orders of battle 5

Ordnance Board, Ordnance Office see
  Board of Ordnance

Ordnance Survey 44, 45

Organization

Army 2, 3, 4, 5, 54
  Battalions 4, 5
  Cavalry regiments 5
  Regiments 2, 3, 4, 5

Other ranks
  Birth records 19, 22, 24
  Casualty returns 4, 7, 51
  Colonial and dominion forces 34, 35,
    36, 37
  Courts martial 32
  Death records 18, 20, 23
  Discharges 18, 19
  Families 19, 24
  First World War 47
  Foreign troops in British pay 20, 38,
    39
  India 33, 34
  Marriage records 20
  Militia 20, 28, 29
  Ordnance Survey 44, 45
  Pensions 18, 19, 22, 23, 24, 74, 75
  Royal Artillery 20, 25, 26
  Royal Engineers 20, 27
  Service records 18, 19, 24, 70, 71, 72
  Soldiers' documents 18, 19
  Wives 18, 20, 21
  see also Soldiers' documents

Out-pensions see pensions

P

Palestine
  First World War 49
  Quarterly Historical Reports 53
  Registers of baptisms and banns of
    marriage 6
  War diaries 53
Peninsular Medal 30

Pensions
  Board of Ordnance 44
  Children and dependent
    relations 16, 48
  Civilian employees 41
  Colonial and dominion forces 35
  Commissariat Department 41
  Disability 24, 48
  Drouly's Annuities 16
  First World War 48
  Foreign troops in British pay 39
  Indian 33
  In-pensions 22, 23, 24
  Militia 28

Nurses 43
Officers 15, 16,
Other ranks 18, 19, 22, 23, 24
Out-pensions 19, 22, 23, 24
Paid abroad 24
Returns 23
Royal Artillery 26
Sappers and Miners 27
Widows 16, 24
Wounds 15, 16

Poland
Free Poles service records 40
Polish Resettlement Corps 40
Polish unit war diaries 39

Presbyterian chaplains 40

Prisoners of war
American War of Independence 45
Crimea 45
First World War 45
Korea 46
Napoleonic wars 45
Second World War 33, 45, 46
South African War (1899-1902) 45

Q

Quarterly Historical Reports 53

Queen Alexandra's Imperial Military
Nursing Service 43

Queen Alexandra's Royal Army Nursing
Corps 43

Queen Mary's Army Auxiliary Corps 50

Queen Mary's Auxiliary Ambulance Corps
48, 50

Queen's South Africa Medal 30, 43

R

Ranks
Army 5
Officers 9, 10, 55
Other ranks 17, 57

Regiments
Histories 60

Local record office holdings 59
Location 4, 5, 10, 18
Museums 61
Organization 2, 3, 4, 5
Service records 14
see also under individual regiments

Retired pay 15

Rhode Island
Militia units 36

Rhodesia
Campaign medal 30
Second World War 36

Rifle Brigade 6

Rolls of honour
First World War 48

Roman Catholic chaplains 40

Roundheads 9

Royal African Company 35

Royal African Corps 35

Royal Air Force
Births, marriages and deaths 61
Courts martial 33
see also Royal Flying Corps

Royal Army Medical Corps 2, 43

Royal Artillery
Appointments 25
Baptism records 6
Birth records 25
Casualty returns 26
Death records 7, 25
Deserters 26
Half pay 25
Marriage records 6, 25
Muster rolls 20, 25
Officers 11, 25
Other ranks 25, 26
Pensions 26
Soldiers' documents 25

Royal Bounty 16

Royal Canadian Rifles 35

Royal Dublin Fusiliers 60

Royal Engineers
Appointments 26
Birth records 45
Commissions 26
Death records 7, 27, 44, 45
Half pay 27
Marriage records 27, 45
Muster rolls 20, 27
Officers 11, 26, 27, 44
Other ranks 27, 44, 45
Soldiers' documents 27
Supply and Service Department 27

Royal Flying Corps 49, 50
see also Royal Air Force

Royal Garrison Regiment 14, 42

Royal Hibernian Military School 46

Royal Horse Artillery 25
Baptism and marriage records 6, 26
Description books 26
Service records 26

Royal Hospital Chelsea
Baptism, marriage and burial
records 6
In-pensioners 23, 24, 29
Out-pensioners 19, 22, 23, 24
Pensions 22

Royal Hospital Kilmainham
In-pensioners 23
Out-pensioners 19, 22
Pensions 22

Royal Irish Artillery 26

Royal Irish Regiment 60

Royal Lancers 60

Royal Marines 21, 46

Royal Military Academy 47

Royal Military College 47

Royal Munster Fusilliers 60

Royal Red Cross Medal 43

Russia
First World War 49

S

Salonika (Greece)
First World War 49

Sappers and Miners, Royal Corps of
Death records 27
Description books 27
Muster rolls 27
Pensions 27
Service records 27
Soldiers' documents 27

Savoy Hulks 21

School of Military Engineering 27

Schools and colleges 46, 47
see also under individual Schools and
Colleges

Scutari Depot (Crimea)
Muster rolls 20

Second World War
Casualty returns 51, 60, 61
Colonial and dominion forces 36, 51
Death records 61
Home guard 52
Indian Army 34
Medals and awards 52
Nurses 44, 52
Prisoners of War 45, 46
Service records 51
War diaries 39, 51, 52
Women 52

Service records
First World War 47
India 34
Medical staff 42, 43
Militia 28, 29
Officers 10, 11, 13, 14, 17, 28, 34
Other ranks 18, 19, 24
Royal Artillery 25
Royal Engineers 27
Royal Horse Artillery 26
Sappers and Miners 27
Second World War 50, 51
Veterans 42

Shanghai (China)
War diaries 53

Shorncliffe and Hythe (Kent)
Registers of births 6

Sierra Leone
Campaign medal 30
Casualty rolls 7

Silver War Badge 48

Soldiers' documents 18, 19, 21, 24
Colonial and dominion forces 34, 36
King's German Legion 38
Medical staff 43
Militia 29
Royal Artillery 25
Royal Engineers 27
Sappers and miners 27
Veterans 42

Somaliland
Campaign medal 30

Somerset Light Infantry 6

South Africa
Emigration 39
National Archives of South Africa
holdings 37
Service records 37
South African Constabulary 37

South African War (1878-1881)
Casualty returns 7
Medals 30
Siege of Lydenburg 14

South African War (1899-1902)
Casualty returns 7, 36, 61
Local volunteer forces 36
Medals 30
Mentions in despatches 31
Nurses 43
Prisoners of war 45
Siege of Ladysmith 14

South Carolina
Loyalist militia 37

Special Services 52

Sudan
Campaign medals 30

Casualty rolls 7
Suez
War diaries 53

Surgeons 42

Surrey Yeomanry 60

Survey companies 44, 45

Switzerland
Troops in British pay 38, 39

T
Territorial and auxiliary forces
associations 59

Territorial Force War Medal 48

Tower Hamlets Militia 29

Trieste (Italy), British Element
Quarterly Historical Reports 53

Tsingtao (China)
Casualty returns 7
Medal rolls 30

Tunisia
Second World War 51

Twentieth century campaigns
Casualty returns 60
War diaries 53

U
Unattached pay 14

Unit Historical Record 53

V
Valenciennes (France)
Prisoners of war 45

Veterans
Battalions 42
Casualty returns 42
Foreign Veterans Battalion 39
Muster rolls 42
Royal Corps of Invalids 42
Service records 42
Soldiers' documents 42

Victoria Cross (VC) 31, 52, 59, 77

Victory Medal 48

Voluntary Aid Detachments (VAD) 44, 50

Volunteer Officers' Decoration 30

W

War diaries 55, 79
    Colonial and dominions forces 36
    First World War 49
    Indian Army 34
    Second World War 36, 39, 41, 52
    Twentieth century campaigns 53

War Office
    Boy Messenger Friendly Society 41
    Civilian employees 41
    War Office List 11, 41
    War Office School 41

Waterloo Medal 29

Waterloo (Belgium)
    Battle 14, 38, 39

Weslyan chaplains 40

West Africa
    Garrisons 35
    Quarterly Historical Reports 53
    War diaries 52

West India Rangers 35

West India Regiments 35

West Norfolk Regiment 6

Westminster Dragoons 60

Widows' pensions **see** pensions

Wills 8, 16

Women
    First World War 50
    Second World War 52
    Service before 1914 21
    see also Nurses

Woolwich (Kent)
    Hospital 43

Y

Yeomanry 28, 29

Yorkshire Rifles 6